Prayer Warrior

Confessions

Compiled By:
Harriet E. Michael
&
Shirley Crowder

Shirley Crowder
1 Thessalonians 5:11

Pix-N-Pens Publishing

Prayer Warrior Confessions

© Copyright 2018 Harriet E. Michael and Shirley Crowder

ISBN: 978-1-944120-60-3

Published by:

Pix-N-Pens Publishing
PO Box 702852
Dallas TX 75370

Find out more about authors, Harriet E. Michael and Shirley Crowder at their author pages at www.WriteIntegrity.com.

Printed in the United States of America

Acknowledgments

We, the authors, are grateful for our Nigeria Missionary Kid cousin, Baker Hill, who provided input and expertise in helping get this manuscript ready for publication.

We are grateful to our publisher, Marji Laine Clubine, for her encouragement, advice, and guidance throughout the process of writing and publishing this anthology, and for the beautiful cover design. We appreciate Karen Jurgens Harrison for her invaluable editing skills.

Table of Contents

Dedication

We dedicate this book to the many prayer warriors
who have prayed for us throughout our lives.

Introduction

from Harriet:

Call to Me and I will answer you, and I will tell you great and mighty things, which you do not know. Jeremiah 33:3 NASB

In Jeremiah 33:3, God tells us to call to Him and He will answer. When my youngest son, Ty, was in a private Christian elementary school, he climbed in the car one afternoon during carpool pick-up, exclaiming, "Mom, I know God's phone number!"

Ty went on to explain that God's phone number was Jeremiah 33:3. This was the way this passage had been taught to him that day—as God's phone number. The concept made me smile. God has a phone number and His line is never busy. When we call to Him, we never have to leave a message. Although it may sometimes feel like we are leaving a message and waiting for Him to get back with us, we are not. God hears us each and every time we pray.

from Shirley:

Rejoice always, pray without ceasing, in everything give thanks; for this is the will of God in Christ Jesus for you. 1 Thessalonians 5:16-18 (ESV)

My parents and countless others demonstrated how to rejoice always and pray without ceasing. I love to hear accounts of God answering the prayers of His people.

This book is part of a four-book collection on prayer. The anchor books in the collection provide a thorough study of prayer from the New and Old Testaments: *Prayer: It's Not About You* written by Harriet, and, *Study Guide on Prayer—A Companion to Prayer: It's Not About You by Harriet E. Michael* written by me. The third book in the collection is a devotional Harriet and I co-wrote, *Glimpses of Prayer*." Pix-N-Pens Publishing produced the entire collection.

from Harriet & Shirley:

This book is a collection of stories of personal experiences with prayer. Many of the stories were written by Harriet or Shirley, and there are also stories in this collection by other prayer warriors. All of the stories are true. The book is a nonfiction work containing real stories of Christ-followers' experiences with prayer. In each case, the person, whom we are calling a prayer warrior, shares a lesson of some kind that he or she learned. These lessons are the prayer warrior's personal testimony of what he or she learned about prayer through the experience. Each story ends with "My Confession" by that Prayer Warrior. We hope you are blessed by them all.

*And just a note: both Harriet and Shirley, the compilers of this book, spent many childhood days in Nigeria, West Africa, as children of missionaries. Because of this, there is a strong Nigerian connection in many of the stories contained in this book. Some were written by Harriet and Shirley and tell of things that happened in Nigeria, some were written by other childhood friends of the compilers and pertain to Nigeria, and some were written by Nigerian friends of the authors as well.

✝

~ A Heritage of Prayer ~

The boundary lines have fallen for me in pleasant places;
surely I have a delightful inheritance. Psalm 16:6 (NIV)

1
The Faith of My Father

My father was a man of prayer.

He knelt by his bedside every night before he crawled in his bed, and he prayed. Some nights when I was a child, if I happened to get up for some reason, or those times when I came in late as a teenager, I'd catch a glimpse of him in his pajamas, kneeling by his bed, praying.

I have a distinct memory of this from my teenage years. My dad was a beloved physician in a small West Virginia city in those days. I was proud to be known as his daughter. One night as I tiptoed past my parents' room on the way to my room, I saw him there, in his pajamas, on his knees … like a little boy. The image was precious to me then, and more precious to me now. Here was a man who gave medical orders that others followed. A man respected by all who knew him. A man who sometimes held other people's lives in his hands as he performed life-saving surgery on them. Yet he humbled himself before God the same way he had since childhood.

My father was a brilliant man who seemed to know something about everything—at least his children thought so. One of my favorite stories about my father's expertise as a physician happened in Nigeria, when another physician was about to perform a Cesarean section on a woman who was post-term but had shown no signs of labor. Before he started, he inserted a syringe into her abdomen as part of the procedure. The fluid he withdrew did not look like what he had expected to find. The surgeon, Dr. Connell Smith, called for my father to consult with him and asked what could possibly give such a finding. My father thought a minute. Then shaking his head, he said, "Well, the only thing I can think of would be an abdominal pregnancy."

An abdominal pregnancy is an extremely rare type of an ectopic pregnancy where the baby grows outside the uterus in the abdominal cavity. This type of pregnancy is dangerous for both mother and baby and most of the babies do not survive such a pregnancy. A few do thrive, but cannot be delivered in the normal way, since the baby is not in the uterus.

Dr. Smith laughed at my father in a teasing manner; they were actually very close friends. He said that was not a plausible answer since the odds of having an abdominal pregnancy were so incredibly slim. My father cautioned his friend, just the same, recommending extreme precaution be used when making the initial incision—because there might be a baby just beneath the abdominal wall.

Dr. Smith asked my dad to perform the C-Section instead because Daddy was better trained in this particular type of surgery, and there were other surgeries that Dr. Smith could be doing.

As my father scrubbed in for the case, Dr. Smith dropped out and made preparations to work elsewhere. My father began to carefully make his incision before Dr. Smith had gone very far. As the incision was made, there before my father's eyes, just under the abdominal wall, was a pulsating umbilical cord. Daddy held up the surgery for just a minute and told one of the operating room assistants, "Quick! Go call Dr. Smith!"

My father was also a loving and gentle man. If it's true that a child gets her first mental image of God by looking at her father, it's no wonder I have always seen my Heavenly Father as a faithful and loving God. Once as a child, my doll broke. In those days, toys were hard to come by in Nigeria. Most were shipped in barrels from the States along with our other belongings. They needed to last until our next furlough. A broken toy could rarely be replaced.

When the barrels were opened, my treasured doll was headless, as its head had fallen off in shipment. It may sound funny now, but it was a real tragedy at the time. I was a middle child with sisters on either side of me. Both of their dolls weathered the trip and arrived in perfect condition, but my doll was headless! My father told me not to cry; he was a doctor, and he put broken people back together all the time.

He took my doll and me to the hospital on a Saturday afternoon when it was not very busy. There, he put a surgical gown and mask on me and donned one himself. He laid my doll on an operating table and sewed her head back on with surgical thread. As promised, my baby was healed. She had some obvious stitches in her neck, but she was put back together just the same. My dad took us home with "doctor's orders" for my doll to take it easy for a couple of days, and he let me keep the surgical mask.

But it's my father's walk with the Lord that I admired most. He feared God and he prayed powerfully.

After twelve years on the mission field, my father began to

feel the Lord calling us out of missions and back to service for Him in the States. Daddy said he felt as called out of foreign mission work as he had felt called to it. My mother objected. They agreed together to pray about it.

Several occurrences happened about the same time, including the onset of the Biafran War. We experienced a few years of the war before leaving the mission field.

I recall one particular time when my father was asked to relieve a doctor at the hospital in Eku. The missionaries had been evacuated from Eku because it was so close to the fighting. In an effort to keep the hospital open, the doctors were asked to staff it for two weeks at a time. During the two weeks my father was there, my mother kept busy during the days working as the Operating Room supervisor at the hospital in Ogbomoso where we lived.

Every night she would take my younger sister and me to the hospital and radio my father in Eku. I remember hearing his voice on the two-way radio. It seemed like a great adventure until time came to end the call. Every night my mom's voice quaked as she fought back tears before saying goodbye. The intensity of my mother's emotion told me that this was not a fun adventure.

In addition to the danger on the home front, there were the older children at the boarding school to worry about in a time of war. The concerns were real, so my mother finally told my father, "Stop praying! You've started a war!" He teased back that she had started the war by not listening to him in the first place.

My Confession: *I learned to pray at the feet of my father.*

~ Harriet E. Michael ~

2
No Ordinary Woman

My mother was born in rural North Carolina in a small wooden house her father had built with his own hands. He was a farmer with only a third-grade education. He supported his wife, four children, and two old-maid aunts with the money he earned working in a textile mill and from the sale of the crops he grew on his farm. My mother's two older brothers quit school after the sixth grade in order to work in the mills and help support the family. My mom, Alice, was the first person in her family to ever graduate from high school.

After high school, Alice attended a nursing school at a nearby hospital. For one of the years of her nursing program, the students went to Winston-Salem to train in their larger hospitals. While there, she met my father, Keith. He was a young medical student whose father and grandfather had also been doctors. He was smitten by this tall, slim brunette with deep blue eyes. As their relationship developed, the time came for him to meet her family.

My grandfather was beside himself with worry in the days

prior to Keith's arrival. He was embarrassed by his humble home which still did not have indoor plumbing. He told her, "That young doctor will take one look at this place and turn around and leave … and never come back."

Maintaining her composure Alice responded with absolute certainty, "If he does, then he's not the man I want anyway."

I've always loved that story. And I've always loved my mother's determination and can-do attitude. There is no task too difficult for my mother to not at least attempt it.

She learned to sew as a teenager. Luxuries were rare and money for extra clothes was nonexistent. But, cow feed came in pretty cotton prints which people often used as cloth to make new clothes. Alice eagerly learned how to sew using the feed bags, making new dresses for her younger sister and herself. Thus began a life of sewing garments for others. She sewed my wedding dress as well as my sisters' wedding dresses and her own. Her talent came in very handy when my family lived in Nigeria.

One of my missionary aunts told me about a special outfit Mom had once sewn for her. Marie had to leave Nigeria with her family quite suddenly due to an illness. She spoke to Mom just a couple of days before she left the mission station. Marie lamented the fact that the only outfit she had to travel in was the one she wore when she came to Nigeria many years earlier. The material was worn and the fit was no longer quite right, but it was all she had for the cooler temperatures she would encounter as she traveled out of Africa. A complaint like that in front of my mom was like throwing red meat in front of a hungry animal—Alice was all over it. She pulled out patterns, material, scissors, pins, and a tape measure that she had brought over in the crates and had carefully stored away. Some of the cloth was thicker and perfect for international travel back to a colder climate. Alice worked all through the night and into the next day so that Marie could wear a lovely new outfit a few days later as she boarded the plane for the USA.

Of all the things my mother has ever sewn, perhaps her greatest challenge came while in Nigeria, with the death of a fellow missionary, Dr. Connell Smith. Dr. Smith was a surgeon at the hospital where both of my parents worked. He was a friend and colleague in the workplace to my mother and was an especially close friend to my father. His death was sudden—the result of an automobile accident. His service and burial were at the chapel of the mission hospital where both of my parents worked. The hospital carpenter made a casket for him out of local wood and my mother sewed its lining out of soft blue satin material that she had brought with her to Nigeria.

Mom told me once that when she saw the blue satin material in a fabric store while on furlough in the USA, it caught her eye. She felt sort of silly buying it and packing it in the crates destined for Nigeria. She kept thinking there would never be any reason to use the material. After all, who needed an elegant blue satin dress in rural Africa in the 1960s? But something seemed to compel her to buy it—almost like she heard God whisper that she would be using this material in Nigeria for a very special event.

And so, that rough casket, made by the skillful hands of a Nigerian carpenter who loved Dr. Smith, was padded and lined by the equally skillful hands of my mother, a woman who also loved him. This dedicated man who lost his life in the foreign country where God had called him, was laid to rest beneath the African soil that he loved with the help of people who loved him.

Proverbs 31:28 says, *Her children arise and call her blessed;*

her husband also, and he praises her. (NIV) This has come true for my mother. We, her children, call her blessed and my father has spent his life praising her. She was a doer of God's Word and not just a hearer.

I never saw her praying by her bed, like I saw my father, but I know she was a woman of prayer. I credit her many earnest prayers for keeping me, and others she loved, constantly held up before the throne of the Almighty.

> ***My Confession:*** *I hope I can be half the caring, ministering woman my mother is, and I hope I can hear God's nudging, too.*
> ~ Harriet E. Michael ~

3
Faith in A Foreign Land

God has surrounded me with faithful people, even from my earliest days. In Nigeria, I knew many brave Christians, some whose faithfulness cost them dearly.

Reverend Paul Ogunyele pastored Oja Oba Church, the church I attended as a child. Being fluent in the Yoruba language, my parents joined this Yoruba-speaking church instead of the English-speaking one nearby, where most of the American missionary families attended. From my earliest memories, I have known this man's story.

Born into a typical Nigerian family of that time, Rev. Ogunyele grew up in a pagan and Muslim household. Members of his large, extended family practiced these two religions, yet they allowed him to attend a Christian school in order to gain an education. He gained more than that—he learned about Jesus' sacrifice for his sins and accepted Jesus as his Savior and Lord. The day he made his profession of faith in Jesus as a twelve-year-old boy, he excitedly ran home to share his joy with his family.

Sadly, his family did not receive the news well.

His family, like many Nigerians at that time, held certain superstitions, and one of these centered around the number three. To their way of thinking, three was an evil number. The men held a family meeting and discussed the danger they believed existed if their family practiced three religions. After much discussion, they decided with certainty that young Paul could not be allowed to be a Christian. They believed the safety and well-being of the entire family rested on that choice.

The next day, the family elders informed Paul that he must renounce his new-found faith. Paul refused, causing the family elders to raise the stakes. They informed him that having three religions in their family would surely bring destruction to every member and they simply could not allow it. He could choose either of the other religions—Paganism or Islam—but not Christianity. If he continued to refuse to renounce his Christian faith, they would have no choice but to kill him.

That night, while the family slept, twelve-year-old Paul Ogunyele climbed out his window and ran away from home. He truly forsook everything for the sake of the cross. And it was my honor to have known such a man and to have grown up calling him, "Pastor."

Owudi felt like a second mother to me. I do not know her full name; I always just called her Owudi. She became my nanny when I was just a newborn. At the time, my parents worked in Joinkrama, a jungle village in the Niger River delta.

Shortly before my birth, Owudi became a Christian. Her

abusive, pagan husband angrily divorced her and sent her away, telling her to never come back. In that place and time, a woman had few rights. Owudi had no lawyers to hire, no judges to hear her appeal. Her only choice was to renounce her faith in Jesus and stay in her marriage, or walk away, losing everything including contact with her three small children, but keeping her faith. She kept her faith.

God gained a saint and I gained a loving, tender, second mother.

Rev. Asaju served as the chaplain of the hospital where both of my parents worked. He was ordained, a high honor among Nigerian pastors, and an honor many did not have. It took years of service before a pastor earned the distinction of becoming ordained.

When I was eight years old, I made a profession of faith in a chapel service at Vacation Bible School, which was always held during our annual mission meeting. My parents informed my pastor, Reverend Ogunyele, of my decision the next Sunday at church. He rejoiced with us, arranged to come to my home to question me to assess my decision and to counsel me if I had questions, but he could not baptize me because he was not yet ordained.

Many missionary kids were baptized by their pastor-fathers at the English-speaking church. However, because my father was a doctor and not a pastor he was also not ordained, prohibiting him from baptizing me according to our denominational guidelines. He also strongly desired that I be baptized by a Nigerian, so he asked

Rev. Asaju to baptize me. And that is how I—an eight-year-old, white American child—came to be welcomed into the family of God in a baptismal service in a Yoruba-speaking church by a black, Nigerian pastor.

A few weeks later, my father received this letter (typed on hospital stationery and recorded here exactly as it was written).

Ogbomoso Baptist Hospital
P.O. Box 15
11/12/67

Dear Dr. & Mrs. T. K. Edwards,

The occasion of yesterday afternoon was one of those I will never forget in my life for the meaning it has for me and for the course of Christ in this land.

Your daughter was the first American missionary I had the privilege to baptize. The most important thing about it is this—that oneness in Christ you preach is practicalized. That is you prove to us that you do not say by mouth that you may love the Nigerians but you demonstrate it. May the love of Christ continue to flow through you to many in this land as you dedicate your lives for the service of our Lord. Amen.

I am,
Yours sincerely,
D. A. Asaju

My Confession: Many have shaped my spiritual life and my prayers as they demonstrated through their lives their genuine faith in a real God; a faith worth forsaking everything to gain. Memories of these brave African men and women still inspire and encourage me and I am humbled to realize that as a child, in some small way, I was an encouragement to them.

~ Harriet E. Michael ~

4
Neither Will Survive

My maternal grandparents, Callie Hudson Thomason and Richard Olin Thomason, had nine children. My mom was number eight of the nine. Grandmother and Granddaddy made certain their children attended church, learned to read their Bibles, and prayed. Grandmother Callie was a prayer warrior. When the Lord laid a person or situation on her heart she prayed diligently.

In 1924, Grandmother became pregnant with her eighth child—my mother, Jeannie. In May of 1925, just six weeks away from my Mom's due date, Grandmother grew so ill that an ambulance had to be called to transport her to the hospital. In those days, ambulances were manned mostly by volunteers who had been trained only in First Aid. Coming into a home to face someone as seriously ill as my grandmother was probably quite foreboding for them.

My Aunt Roberta, 95 at the time I am writing this account, has two memories of that traumatic event which occurred when she was only four-years-old. She remembers the men carrying her mother out of the house on a stretcher to the waiting ambulance. They had placed a handkerchief over my grandmother's face, but no one seems to remember why. Perhaps they did not want her seven watching children to see the pain and agony on their mother's face, fearing it would cause them unnecessary concern. Though concern was surely merited, there was no need to frighten the children at that point in time.

To the seven children watching their mom being carried out on a stretcher, the handkerchief over her face seemed alarming, not comforting. So frightening that even at the age of four, Aunt Roberta remembers these things with surprising clarity ninety-one years later.

Dr. Lex Hubbard, long-time Thomason family doctor, was both a wonderful doctor and a strong Christ-following man. He admitted Grandmother to the hospital, where he, with grave concern etched on his face, advised the expectant couple that my grandmother needed immediate gall bladder surgery, even though it would likely cost the baby—my mom—her life. The doctors did not expect the baby to survive the surgery. My grandmother gave her consent for surgery, requesting two things of the doctors: "First of all, do everything you can to safeguard the life of my unborn baby; and, pray diligently that I will recover and return home to my family."

Both doctors were Christ-followers and spoke reassuringly to her. Dr. Hubbard said, "My dear, we know that you desire to get well so you can continue caring for your seven children who are at home awaiting your return. Rest assured that we will pray and do everything we know to do to enable God to answer our prayers."

Granddaddy and Dr. Hubbard stood in that small hospital room and prayed together, asking the Lord to guide the hands of the surgeons and to give the surgical team wisdom, discernment, and skill beyond themselves to perform a successful surgery. They asked that if it was in God's will, that He would be pleased to spare the lives of my grandmother and her unborn child.

The reliance upon the Lord, the medical knowledge and skill of the doctors and medical team, and the prayerful vigilance of a faithful husband were rewarded.

My grandmother not only survived the surgery, but thrived, as did the baby—my mother—who was still safe in my grandmother's womb. Six weeks later, Grandmother gave birth to her eighth child and fifth daughter, Imogene Gertrude, whom everyone fondly called Jeannie.

And, two years later, Grandmother gave birth to her ninth and last child, her sixth daughter, Betty Eloise. My grandmother lived another forty-seven years serving the Lord and caring for her family. Granddaddy and Grandmother provided a Christian home where they faithfully raised their children in the fear and admonition of the Lord. The resulting nine Christian families included three in vocational Christian service.

Some thirty years after her birth, my mom and dad prepared to answer God's call to the mission field as foreign missionaries to Nigeria, West Africa. Before leaving the States, Mom made it a point to drop by Dr. Hubbard's office and tell him she was heading to Africa to be a missionary. He responded to the news with, "Well, I'm not surprised. God definitely answered our prayers by saving your mom's life and yours. He saved you for a reason, and now we know that reason."

Mom loved the Nigerian people, and as she befriended them, she taught them how to sew and to cook American foods while they taught her to cook Nigerian foods, and she taught them the

Word of God by demonstrating how to live out faith in Him.

For the balance of her life, my mom took seriously God's command to make disciples of all those with whom she came in contact. Everyone who knew her loved her, and they understood that she cared for them. God chose to save my mother's life even before she was born.

I have a great family heritage of people who were, and are, fervent prayer warriors. We have seen the Lord work in and through my family's prayers in the lives of countless people in Nigeria, the States, and the entire world. Had it not been for the faithful prayers of others (family, friends, and Christ-followers), my mom might have never been born. And, that skinny buck-toothed girl from Alabama would have never influenced innumerable people for the Gospel all over the world throughout her eighty-six years of life. Her ministry continues today through the lives of my family and others throughout the world.

My Confession: God's ways are not our ways. Sometimes when we are praying for a specific situation, God has a much bigger plan in mind which will bear fruit for years to come.
~ Shirley Crowder ~

~ Prayer that Availeth Much ~

Confess your faults one to another, and pray one for another, that ye may be healed. The effectual fervent prayer of a righteous man availeth much.
James 5:16 (KJV)

5
Moses Nwoke

Like the Moses in the Bible, Moses Nwoke nearly lost his life shortly after birth. Also like the biblical Moses, this Moses' birth occurred near a river. But that's where the similarities end.

Moses Nwoke was born in a small village in eastern Nigeria, in the delta area of the Niger River in the early 1940's. His mother died giving birth to him. His village held a superstitious belief about babies like Moses. Steeped in black magic, the villagers thought a baby whose mother died while giving birth was possessed with an evil spirit. This, they reasoned, was why the mother had died—the evil spirit in the baby had killed the mother. The mother's death alone was sufficient evidence of the existence of this evil spirit in the eyes of the people who inhabited remote villages like his back in those days.

The village had a solution to this type of problem. They threw babies like Moses in the nearby Niger River to rid the village of the evil spirit while at the same time appeasing their gods. They assumed one of their pagan gods had sent this evil spirit out of anger and the villagers hoped the sacrificed child would calm the angry god and they would again have peace in the village.

Newborn Moses would have had his fate sealed at birth because of something completely out of his control, the tragic death of his mother, were it not for a group of Christian women who lived in a nearby village. These women knew the practice of child sacrifice was wrong. They understood the value of created life because they knew the Creator. These women had a practice of their own. As soon as they heard of a maternal death, they hurried to the scene before the villagers had time to throw the baby to his death. They asked these villagers to give them the babies who would otherwise have been doomed to a watery grave— babies like Moses. These women even renamed their little village "Graveyard" (or rather the native word that meant graveyard). By doing so, the women could assure the neighboring villagers they could still appease their gods and be rid of the evil spirit by honestly telling their gods that the baby in question had been sent to the "graveyard."

Moses Nwoke was one of the first babies saved by this group of dedicated Christian women. He grew up in Graveyard reared by these precious women. Moses had over a dozen mothers pouring their love on him and teaching him about the God who had great plans for his life and about that God's Son, Jesus.

My parents came to know Moses when he was a young man. To them, he was one of the first and most trustworthy nurses at the little hospital in Joinkrama, Nigeria, where they served as medical missionaries in the late 1950s—the same hospital where I was born.

After some time, however, Moses rather abruptly quit his job at the village hospital where my parents worked, taking another more lucrative job with one of the international oil companies drilling in the oil-rich Niger River Delta. My parents were sad to see him go. They had grown quite fond of Moses. His new company moved him away from Joinkrama to the larger city of Benin City.

A few years later, my father received a letter from Moses. In this letter, Moses said he had become quite prosperous. He told of living in an air-conditioned building with an electric light bulb in his room. For the first time in his life, he was now sleeping in a real bed with a pillow and sheets. He had other furniture in his room, too—a desk and a chair. But Moses also confessed that he had wandered away from his faith in the years since he left his home village and the people who loved him. He said he had stopped attending church and had even ceased reading his Bible. Then, as his letter continued, he told this experience. He wrote that one night, while sitting on his chair in his air-conditioned room, he noticed his Bible among the belongings that he had brought with him and he decided to open it. This, he confessed, was the first time he had opened his Bible in a very long time.

That night, by divine providence, Moses said he just happened to turn in his Bible to Mark 8:36. As his eyes fell on the passage in front of him, he read *What good is it for someone to gain the whole world, yet forfeit their soul?* (NIV) This verse pierced Moses' heart. His letter said he looked around at his comfortable environment. He first noticed his bed with sheets and a pillow, then the electric light by which he was able to read, even at night, and his desk and chair. He said he had things he'd never dreamed of before. He hadn't even known such things existed, much less ever imagined owning them when he was a child growing up in Graveyard.

34

That night Moses realized what really mattered in life. He finally understood for the first time what held real value in this world. It was not clean sheets or modern technology. And it was not air-conditioned rooms which could keep a person comfortable even in Africa. He remembered the women who had risked their lives to save him because they knew the value of life. Oh, how they had sacrificed for him and then spent their lives loving him. These women had done this because saving a person and ultimately saving a soul was what really counted in life.

Moses bowed his head to pray. He asked God to forgive him for leaving the faith these dear women had instilled in him since he'd been a child. He re-committed his life to the Lord and asked God to allow him to make a difference to others the way these women had made a difference in his life.

With this new perspective, Moses left his lucrative job with the oil company and went back to working as a nurse in an area near his little village of Graveyard.

In his later years, he served as the head nurse of the pediatric department of Methodist Hospital in a city called Ilesha. Here he contributed greatly to curing the problem of kwashiorkor in children. This is a condition that results from a protein deficiency due to malnutrition. Malnutrition and its subsequent complications were serious problems in this part of the world at that time because of both the lack of healthy food as well as the people's lack of nutritional understanding. They did not know what was necessary for good nutritional health for them or their children. Children suffered the most as their little bones and bodies were undergoing such rapid growth, and the need for protein was so significant.

And so, in the end, Moses Nwoke spent his life helping sick and malnourished children. This man, who was rescued as a baby by a group of believing women, spent his life rescuing other children from sickness and death and then lovingly restoring them to health.

> ***My Confession:*** *God answered Moses's prayer abundantly. God is in the business of answering prayer and making something out of the lives of His creation.*
>
> ~ Harriet E. Michael ~

6
Praying for My Future

"Maybe you weren't born to be a doctor."

My uncle's words rang in my ears and stung my heart as I once again failed the matriculation examination for admission into the university. My mind wandered back ...

As a ten-year-old boy, I dreamed of becoming a doctor. When asked what career path I would like to pursue, I never hesitated to let everyone know that I would go into the medical field—I would someday become a doctor. I held fast to this dream in the years that followed. It became an obsession that was inseparable with who I was. In my mind, I pictured myself in my white coat—always adorned in the attire of a doctor. Together with some friends, enraptured by the same great desire, we formed an alliance to assiduously bring this dream to pass.

On graduation from high school, I sat for my first matriculation examination, but, sadly, I did not make the grade. I decided to re-sit the following year but the second attempt was also unsuccessful. My family became anxious and distraught. Most of my high school friends who had long shared my same aspirations were already offered provisional admission into the university of their choice. I felt like the odd sheep among my pack of friends. The idea my uncle put in my head started blurring my vision. I quietly started believing the lies and deceit of the negative energy he consistently communicated to me.

The following year, I decided to have a third try to gain admission into the university of my choice. My family advised that I should drop medicine and apply for one of the other sciences. But in my mind, I could not let go of my dream, nurtured like a baby for so many years. I sat for the examination once again, having prepared rigorously, but when the results were out, the story wasn't any better. Gloom began to set in, days became long, and it took forever for nights to fall. I began to wonder if I had come to the twilight of my childhood dreams. Yet something in me hesitated to give up. I felt I had no option. I refused to believe that I had wasted all those years attempting to achieve an unattainable goal.

I enrolled in a remedial program at an education center. My passion was still strong, and my nerves were wired with the circuit of determination. Even though the negative voices attempted to have a field day in my mind, I fought with all the strength I could muster. In my peril, I remembered the wisdom of Napoleon Hill that "Whatever the mind can conceive and the heart believe, can be achieved." On many occasions, while I was preparing for my fourth sitting, I stood in front of the mirror and gave myself pep talks. I imagined myself performing medical procedures. The mind battle was intense, the deafening discouraging voices kept reminding me how big and unrealistic my dream was, but one lone positive voice nudged silently to my soul. "You can do it." I read stories of men who attempted a task and failed many times like

Abraham Lincoln and Thomas Edison until they eventually achieved their ultimate goal. Their stories helped fire my passion of persistence and ignite my vision of hope.

And I took to my knees too. I prayed often and earnestly that God would allow me to pass the matriculation exam and gain entrance into a university medical program. After regaining some self-confidence and keeping my eyes focused in faith that God had heard my prayers, I willingly faced the giant once more.

The day approached. I prepared dutifully in this fourth attempt to gain admission. I did the normal rituals of studying and performance evaluation. Satisfied with my practices, I began to see possibility in my seemingly impossible situation. I wrote the examination in high spirits. When the result was released, I found my name on the board for university admission. I was admitted to study Veterinary Medicine. Tears of joy streamed slowly from my eyes and a shout of victory was all I could scream. At last the giant had fallen. God had once again slain Goliath.

During my convocation in 2011, my family was ecstatic. What had seemed impossible had become possible. God proved that nothing is impossible with Him. And my persistence showed that the world stands up for a man who won't give up on his dream.

My Confession: There is an old saying, "God helps those who help themselves." This may not be theologically accurate and there are many times God helps those who cannot help themselves. Often God expects us to do our part too. With prayer and effort, much can be accomplished.

~ Nwakuche Emeka ~

7
Praying for Penny

I stood in line at the grocery store chatting with my friend, Karen, when a familiar name came up. Penny. I hadn't thought about her in years.

"What's she doing now?" I asked. "I heard she was married and living in California."

Karen hesitated. "Um … yes. She moved to Los Angeles to … further her career."

"Oh, what career is that?" Penny had done some modeling in high school. Maybe she was soon to be the next cover girl.

"Oh, Tracy, don't ask me anything else."

What a strange response. I stepped behind my cart and took a sudden interest in the *National Enquirer*.

After a few awkward moments, Karen spoke quietly. "I don't know how to explain it. If you want to see for yourself, go to her website." She leaned over and whispered an address fit for a porn star.

Oh. Now I was getting the picture.

On the way home, I prayed about what to do and decided I did have to see for myself. A short while later, I sat at my computer clicking on screen after screen of my young friend in a variety of sensual and erotic poses. Her bio made it clear she sought auditions for serious acting jobs, but the eight by ten glossies she offered for sale left little to the imagination. If she was looking for exposure, she was certainly getting it. With a heavy heart, I closed my browser.

Penny and my son had gone to kindergarten together. With her mane of rich, brown hair, olive skin, and long lashes, Penny had the attention of all the little boys even then. In later years, she and my son attended the same youth group and Sunday school class. Never would I have pictured her doing something like this.

I was restless for several days and couldn't get Penny off my mind. I kept picturing her as that innocent five-year-old from what seemed like only yesterday. Now she was swimming in murky waters where it would be all too easy for her to drown in her own ambitions. How could she sell herself like that? I picked up the phone to call her and then put it back down, afraid I would say something to alienate her. After much prayerful contention, I finally called.

Our conversation went well, even when I told Penny I had seen her website and was worried about her being exploited. I figured she couldn't be too mad at someone who was genuinely concerned for her. She laughed and said not to worry, that she had everything under control.

I hung up and sighed. At least I had tried. But more days passed, and God began pulling on my heartstrings again. I found some kindergarten pictures of Penny—my thinly-veiled excuse for writing—and mailed them to her. In the accompanying letter, I talked about her dreams of becoming an actress and gently encouraged her to rethink her path to attain them. This time, Penny's response was different. She returned the letter, which had been opened and taped shut again, with a note on the back of the envelope saying, "DO NOT CONTACT ME AGAIN!"

Ouch. Okay, sister.

Penny had shut the door. I would respect her wishes and stop trying to contact her. But she couldn't stop me from praying for her. My campaign began that moment. God directed me to a focal verse, Psalm 38:4: *For mine iniquities are gone over mine head: as an heavy burden they are too heavy for me.* (KJV) I began praying for Penny every night.

Never before nor since have I prayed for anyone other than my own family with such consistency or fervor. Normally, my long-term prayers become rote and repetitious. Not this time. Night after night, God gave me a new objective. I prayed for protection and conviction. I prayed God would align Penny's desires with His and give her a new sense of direction. I prayed her husband would intervene and that God would send someone to speak truth into her life. Each prayer was short and specific. Each one was different. I knocked on heaven's door with pleas and petitions for almost a year.

Then one day, I stopped. As quickly as the urgency to pray came, it left. I hadn't given up on Penny. I just no longer felt the need to pray for her. God gave me a sense of peace, though I regretted that I would never learn the outcome of my prayers.

Three weeks later, my husband pointed out an ad in the local newspaper. "Look at this."

Penny and her husband had moved back to our area and were going into business—a legitimate business—with Penny's mother.

It looked like my young friend wouldn't be an actress, but she wouldn't be exploited either. I later learned she and her husband were raising a family, and I saw indications they were putting God first in their lives.

My attempts to reach out to Penny had failed, but as the Bible says, God's arm is longer than mine. Once again, prayer had proven to be the most powerful catalyst for a changed life.

My Confession: *The effectual fervent prayer of*
a righteous man availeth much. James 5:16b (KJV)
~ Tracy Crump ~

8
Typhus Fever

... In another 24 hours, she would be dead.

Like any six-year-old child, I loved adventures, but none of us were prepared for the adventures we were about to have! Daddy was pastor of a church in Callaway, Florida. Mother worked with women in the church, ministered to families with Daddy and took care of my brother, Paul, and I. Not long after I turned six that January, my parents began preparing Paul and me to become a missionary family. Initially, our parents were told we would serve in China, but soon we learned Nigeria, West Africa would be our new home!

Paul and I were so excited as we traveled to New York City to board the French freighter that would carry us north to St. John's, Canada, then across the Atlantic Ocean for six weeks to Dakar, West Africa. We had to disembark in St. John's for me to have an abscessed tooth removed. From there we sailed those six weeks until we docked in Dakar to take on new passengers and freight. We were all fascinated, and wide-eyed by our first sights, sounds and smells of Africa. Our next stop around the coast of Africa, was Lagos, Nigeria, a large city teeming with people, bicycles, lorries, and cars! After an overnight stay in Lagos, we traveled by car to Oyo where my parents would study Yoruba, the language they expected to become their second language.

As Mother and Daddy studied and struggled to learn this strange, but beautiful language, Paul and I picked up the language quickly as we played with other missionary and Nigerian children. Over the next six months, we came to love Nigeria, her people, the food and the culture. Our best friend became Bolija, a Yoruba teenager who was kicked out of his Muslim home when he became a follower of Jesus. He quickly became a member of our family. He played with us, taught us Yoruba and kept us out of trouble … most of the time.

After six months of study, the Mission assigned my parents to Keffi, a very old but small town with a rich history. It is located not far from Abuja which is now the capital of Nigeria. In the center of the country, Keffi was a town of mostly Hausa-speaking people, with a small group of Yoruba and some Fulani who lived on the outside of town. Until 1960, Nigeria was still a British Colony subject to the Queen of England. This mixture of Nigerian culture with a hint of British culture made it quite unique.

We lived on the mission compound in Keffi just outside of the town. It was a great place to run and play. Our compound was full of all kinds of large and small trees along with thick brush and lots of snakes! We killed 13 cobras our first week in Keffi … in our backyard! Paul and I loved to roam the compound and even venture over the fence to explore. Each night before we took our baths, Mother would check us from head to toe for ticks. Yep, those pesky things that burrow their heads into your skin. My brother Paul was usually the one with several of them, as he was always running through the brush.

During those years, Keffi was a bush town ... a long way from medical care, so our parents took care of us. Periodically, an SIM missionary nurse would come into town to check up on us. Imagine living in a remote town with little to no access to medical treatment.

When I was about eight years old, I began running a very high fever with chills and painful body aches. My fever stayed at 104-105 as my parents tried everything to cool me down. They assumed it was Malaria. One night, after a couple of days of being delirious with such a high fever, I heard my parents whispering their concern. Daddy told Mother, "If her fever doesn't break in two hours (midnight) we will start out for one of the large cities with a hospital."

I drifted off to sleep. That is my first memory of this sickness. I was one very sick girl!

My next memory is waking up in my bed surrounded by Nigerian men dressed in their typical robes, praying fervently out loud in Hausa and Yoruba. I thought I was in heaven and they were angels.

That's all I remember.

My parents told me that at midnight, they began the long and dangerous drive over extremely bad roads to get me to a doctor. Upon arrival, the doctor diagnosed me with Typhus Fever which if left untreated could lead to serious complications and possibility death. The doctor told them my case was quite severe and if they had waited another 24 hours, I would not be alive. The prayers of those precious Nigerian church deacons worked! After treatment and rest, I was totally healed!

Through the years our family, friends, and many churches throughout the USA prayed for my parents daily ... at all hours of the day and night. Please pray for your missionaries and their children!

I thank God for my parents, their love and devotion to God, family, and others!

My Confession: I am grateful for parents, missionary aunts and uncles, and faithful Nigerian Christians who taught me to trust in God by praying and trusting Him in every situation.

~ Anne Crowder Lucas ~

~ God's Still, Small Voice ~

And after the earthquake a fire;
but the LORD was not in the fire:
and after the fire a still small voice. 1 Kings 19:12 (KJV)

9
When My Son Calls

My husband and I have three sons—three fine, upstanding, wonderful sons. And each one of these sons has a different personality. It's not that any one of my sons is any better than the other; they are just quite different. I can see these differences in the way they react or correspond with me and other family members.

The oldest, Ben, is much like me, only better. He and I are alike in that we both sort of resemble lovable, likable, puppies. If a person near us is laughing, we will laugh with him or her. But if crying, and Ben or I are close by, we will surely cry with that sad or grieving person too. We ooze compassion.

This son visits or calls us often, and we can hear the enthusiasm in his voice, "Hello Mom! How are ya? I love ya! Come on, give me a hug. Do you need help with anything? When can I see you? How can I help you?" And as busy as we all are with school and work, we still see this one and his wife, Amanda, as often as possible.

Andy, the youngest, also has a compassionate heart. He and

his growing family like to help out at the various homeless shelters in my area. They bring laughter and smiles to the families there through movie nights. He packs up his wife, Samantha, children, equipment, plus plenty of popcorn and the latest family-friendly flick, and travels to the shelter to share happy moments with homeless people who seem to have few other happy moments in their lives. If you are crying, Andy won't cry with you. No, instead, he will do his best to make you feel better with a smile or a new outlook. Now, this boy is busy. He works all he can to support his growing family. This child of mine, now an adult, is busy making a million dollars one week at a time. We see Andy and family when he has time to spare.

David, our middle son, is also a busy man. Not yet married like his brothers, he works and goes to school. David is our quiet child who we hear from the least. I do not believe he loves us any less, but he just has a quieter way of showing it, which fits his more subdued personality.

But if that young man calls one of us—either my husband or me—we drop everything we are doing and take his call. Why? Because hearing from him is a special treat. We answer his calls and eagerly wait to hear what is on his mind or heart. He might even need us. When David calls, it means he is reaching out to us, and we want to make sure he knows we are available and ready to reach back.

I imagine it must be the same with our Heavenly Father. He eagerly waits to hear from each of us, even though it may have been a long time in between conversations. Or perhaps we just talked to Him moments before—He's still eager to hear what's on our hearts. How overjoyed our Abba Father must be when we reopen communication with Him. I can only imagine, He, too, would drop everything to come and answer our call.

In Matthew 18:12-13, Jesus tells the parable of the good shepherd and the lost sheep. Remember how He left the ninety-nine sheep to search for the one that was lost? He dropped everything to reach out to and help that one who needed Him at that moment. After all, God wants us to know when we reach out to Him, He is already reaching back to us.

Psalm 4:3 says: *But know that the Lord hath set apart him that is godly for himself: the Lord will hear when I call unto him.* (KJV) I love that. The Lord will always hear when I call Him—always, every single time.

Like I know my sons, though they are quite different, God knows each of us with our unique ways too. I hear each of my sons when they call, though they have different personalities and needs. Likewise, God hears each of His children when they call to Him. One person might be the type who calls out to God often, while someone else might be of a quieter nature. God hears each of our calls, every time we pray.

> ***My Confession:*** *God sometimes speaks in a still, small, voice and He eagerly awaits our voice raised in prayer to Him—no matter how still or small our voice may be, too.*
>
> ~ Deborah Aubrey-Peyron ~

10
How Can You Sleep?

A few years ago, I was enjoying a fellowship at a friend's house. Ladies at my church had been gathering weekly for years. A small group of women of all ages met every Wednesday from ten o'clock until noon to have a Bible study led by my friend, Susan, in whose home we met. Most of them were young mothers, but a few of us, like Susan and me, were a bit older. After the Bible study, we always enjoyed a meal together that one of the women had brought.

That day I brought the meal, so I was in the kitchen warming things up and setting the food out on Susan's countertops when I noticed a note card on her refrigerator with a handwritten Bible verse from Jonah 1:6. It read, *"The captain went to him and said, 'How can you sleep? Get up and call on your god! Maybe he will take notice of us so that we will not perish.'"* (NIV)

I thought it an odd verse to have stuck with a magnet to one's refrigerator. People usually display verses that have special meaning, ones that inspire them in some way, often those they wish to memorize. Perhaps Susan or one of her children had been studying the book of Jonah. However, her children were older so not likely to be studying it the way young children might.

"Susan, why do you have this verse on your refrigerator?" I called out to her. She was across the room, helping set out the food. I will never forget her answer.

She walked closer to me and proceeded to tell me something that has stuck in my mind all these years. "Well, that verse rolls around in my head at night, so I decided to write it down and memorize it. I hear it in my mind sometimes in the middle of the night when I wake up. You know how you wake up and just lie there awake wishing so badly that you could go back to sleep?"

I nodded.

"Well," she continued, "a few weeks ago, I had been reading through the Bible in my devotions, and I came across this verse. That night I had one of those times when I woke up suddenly in the middle of the night for no particular reason. And then it happened. This verse popped into my mind with absolute clarity, *'How can you sleep? Get up and call on your God!'* It was almost like God was speaking to me personally, 'Susan! Why are you sleeping? Get up and pray!'"

Susan shook her head and rolled her eyes as she spoke, causing me to laugh.

Without missing a beat, she continued, "So, of course, I figured I better obey. I got up, went to another room so I wouldn't disturb my sleeping husband, whom apparently God hadn't commanded to get up."

She rolled her eyes some more, and I laughed again.

She continued, "And it's happened a few times since then. Actually, it now happens almost every time when I wake up in the middle of the night. That verse pops into my mind and I start praying. I don't get out of bed and go to the other room anymore, but I do wake up and start praying.

I hear God saying, 'How can you sleep? Wake up and call on your God.'

So, I say, 'Okay God. I'm awake, who do you want me to pray for?' Then I think about the people I know and who might need prayer, and I start praying for them. Often people just pop into my mind, so I pray for them even if I don't know their needs."

I stood there soaking in all my friend had said. She peered at me waiting for my response, but I was still digesting what she had said. I must have had a quizzical look on my face because she added, "I mean … what else can I do? I've got to pray if God tells me to, right? I figure God either wakes His people up at night for them to pray for others, or He doesn't. And if He does, then I think this is what it would look like."

My Confession: I sometimes stand amazed at how God works in the lives of other prayer warriors, like my friend Susan. My friend would tell you that her confession is that sometimes God's still, small voice can echo quite loudly in a person's mind and heart.

~ Harriet E. Michael ~

11
I Know the Plans I Have for You

As I lay waiting in the sterile pre-op area of Baylor Hospital in Dallas, many thoughts and images raced through my mind. I nervously anticipated what I would go through the next five hours as I underwent surgery. Rhonda, my wife, sat by my side, providing a calm presence and reassurance, when suddenly a stranger walked up and began talking to me.

I quickly noticed his hospital ID badge, which identified him as a chaplain. But equally as quickly, I recognized his West African accent as soon as he introduced himself. After we exchanged a few greetings, I felt comfortable enough to ask him if he was from West Africa. He didn't hesitate with his answer. He smiled widely and told me he was from the nation of Cameroon. He asked if I was familiar with Cameroon. I said yes and proudly went on to tell him that I knew of Cameroon because it was a country that borders my original homeland, Nigeria. I could tell he was a bit puzzled by my response, so I explained further.

His eyes transitioned from polite interest to delight as I told him about my missionary parents who served in Nigeria and about my birth in the town of Ogbomoso. What had been two complete strangers seconds earlier rapidly turned into a special kinship, the kind that is privileged to only a few.

As our conversation continued, I discovered that he knew the town of my birth quite well since he had once lived there. I quickly found out other things too. My stranger's name was Joseph, and he had been a student at the seminary in Ogbomoso—the town of my birth. What's more, he knew my good friend David. This man, David, had been like a family member to me growing up. To my surprise, I found out that my new chaplain friend had known him as a beloved seminary professor from 1995 to 1998.

Then the man offered to pray for my surgery and recovery. How comforting to know that God had made it possible for such a man to pray for me prior to my surgery. A sense of calm overtook any nervousness and anxiety I had before. I was at peace.

What gave my chaplain friend and me such a strong, and almost instant, bond was more than just a familiarity with each other's homelands. We were brothers in Christ, and as such were joined by a solid and eternal bond. 1 Corinthians 12:13 tells us, ... *we were all baptized by one Spirit so as to form one body—whether Jews or Gentiles* ... (NIV) We are all children of God because of our faith in Christ Jesus. As fellow children of the same Father, my chaplain friend and I knew instantly that we were brothers. Though we were born in separate countries, spoke different native languages, and our skin colors differed, we were children of the same Father and thus brothers, indeed.

My surgery was successful, and I was blessed with a full recovery. Looking back, I continue to be amazed at the power of God and how His hand guides so many in different ways. To think that over fifty years ago a Nigerian named David came to my parents' home as a young uneducated man seeking work. He was first given the task of watching over me, a toddler, and my two older brothers. Later, as he showed more responsibility and interest, my father took David with him to the bush churches where David worked as an interpreter for my father as he preached. Soon David became a Christian himself and went on to dedicate his life to God's work as a pastor and later as a seminary professor in Nigeria.

How could David, Joseph, I, or anyone else know what plan God had made for us so long ago? It was a plan, meticulously made in such a way that only at that particular moment, unannounced to us, would our different worlds instantly intersect and converge as we met one another—the very moment when I needed it most. Why was my surgery scheduled at that particular time? Why was Joseph working that morning? There were other chaplains at the hospital that day, but Joseph came as if he were "assigned" to me. Without a doubt, it was all part of God's plan.

How God worked to bring us together I will never know, but I received a blessing that day as Joseph shared a genuine and heartfelt prayer with me just minutes before my surgery. I cannot help but believe God used Joseph and his connection with my friend David, as well as my missionary parents, to assure all would be well. I enjoyed a bond of brotherhood as I and my situation were lifted up in prayer to my Heavenly Father by a brother. Jeremiah 29:11 says, *"For I know the plans I have for you,"* declares the LORD, *"plans to prosper you and not to harm you, plans to give you hope and a future."* (NIV) I felt a great sense of serenity in knowing God has a plan for us all.

My Confession: God does not always speak to us in obvious ways. That morning God's message to me came through circumstances, through too many "coincidences" to have possibly been just coincidence. As always, God's timing was perfect.

~ Ron Wasson ~

12
Still, Small, Whisper

The verses of 1 Kings 19:11-13 tell the story of a time when the prophet Elijah learned that God doesn't always speak loudly in our lives. Sometimes He speaks in a still, small voice. Can a two-year-old hear this still, small voice of God? Does God sometimes nudge the shoulder of even a preschooler and give him a job to do?

I believe God's voice, even when still and small, can be heard by a child who is only two years old, just about to turn three. After all, in Matthew 19:14 Jesus welcomed little children, pulling them onto His lap and saying, *"Let the little children come to me, and do not hinder them, for the kingdom of heaven belongs to such as these."* (NIV)

My sister, Darlaine, witnessed a little miracle involving her then not quite three-year-old grandson at Vacation Bible School one year and shared the story with me. It happened at a small country church near Columbus, Indiana.

Darlaine's grandson, Xavier, lives with her. She gained custody of him a few years ago after he was removed from his parents' care by Child Protective Services. Under Darlaine's care, he has been loved well and taught about Jesus, even though he was a small child.

Xavier loved the Christian preschool where Darlaine had enrolled him. He attended it during the school year and became quite saddened when summer vacation came and he no longer had daily contact with his school friends. He told "Grandma," as he calls Darlaine, that he missed his friends and knew his friends were missing him, too, and that made him sad.

Darlaine decided to enroll Xavier in the summer VBS at her church. She thought he would enjoy the lessons and the contact with the new friends he made at VBS. Xavier loved Bible school with a passion. They actually did not have a class for two-year-olds or three-year-olds, so they allowed Xavier to join the five-year-old class. Being younger than the others didn't stop him from throwing himself fully into class activities, and he enjoyed it immensely.

Having gone to a Christian preschool, Xavier knew all the answers to the Bible questions and was the first to raise his hand, in spite of his young age. My sister marveled as she watched this once developmentally-delayed baby blossoming into a bright, happy little boy.

Then the special moment happened. It came during the closing of that week's VBS, when the parents gathered together with their children and joined in praying, singing, and celebrating all that the children had learned and accomplished that week.

Another little boy sat on the front pew with his mom, who was signing to him in hand gestures. Xavier watched this for a little while. Then he got up from where he sat, walked up to the front pew, and sat down right next to the little boy, just on the other side from where the mom sat. Xavier turned to the little boy and started making hand motions too.

Darlaine was embarrassed. She thought Xavier was just mimicking the hand motions of the little boy's mother. She ran in a panic to the pew where they all sat and started apologizing to the mother.

The mother said, "Why are you apologizing? Do you know sign language?"

"No" replied Darlaine.

"Do you know what your little boy said to mine?" the mother asked Darlaine.

Darlaine sat stunned, shaking her head "No," she said, "Was he actually saying something with his hand motions?"

The mother's face broke into a warm smile as she happily informed Darlaine, "Your little boy just told my little boy, 'Jesus loves you, and so do I.'"

Darlaine was in utter amazement. She asked Xavier how he knew how to say that in sign language.

Xavier answered with only one word, "Joey."

Then it all made sense to Darlaine. Joey was a deaf child who had been in Xavier's preschool class the year before. The teacher had taught the children how to sign. And every morning she had all the children sign these words to Joey, "Jesus loves you, and so do I."

Yes, I think God sometimes speaks to children. I think when Xavier saw the boy signing with his mother, God tapped him on the shoulder and whispered, "Go tell that little boy that I love him."

And Xavier heard God's whisper and obeyed.

My Confession: We usually think of prayer as us talking to God, but God talks to us, too ... sometimes even telling a two-year-old boy to go over and tell another of His children that He loves him.

~ Laquita Havens ~

~ *Unexpected Answers* ~

His divine power has granted to us all things that pertain to life and godliness, through the knowledge of him who called us to his own glory and excellence.

2 Peter 1:3 (ESV)

13
India's Call

My daughter was in India on a two-month mission trip. Her first week there, she contracted typhoid fever—a strong, life-threatening strain. She was much too weak to go to an Internet café to contact us, and even short phone calls were exorbitant in price. Communication was sparse. We knew she was sick but had few details. Yet, we felt the Lord's grace and peace as we eagerly waited for each new update.

One night at three AM, I sat straight up in my bed with these words on my lips, "Ashli just wrote to me." I went to the computer and found an email from her that had arrived one minute earlier. The Lord must have wanted me to know, for He shook me from a deep sleep.

"Mom, I'm so tired. I can't go on. My body is very weak, I'm so sick. My team is not helpful. I feel like giving up! We will be leaving here soon, to make the next leg of our journey. I do not know if I will be able to make it."

I felt my faith waver as I read her words. What should we do?

If I traveled to India to help bring her home, was she strong enough to make the trip? Was that the path we should take? What other way could we get help to her?

I started trying to contact her by phone but was not able to get through. Discouraged, I went to my place of daily prayer, pulled out my Bible, and pled with the Lord for answers.

I continued to try to call her, every hour, in fact. But it was to no avail. Each time I placed the call only to find that I was not able to get through.

Tears streamed down my face as I pleaded. "Please help, Lord." I cried with everything within me.

Despair teased and twisted my aching heart.

What should I ask God for? I wasn't even sure. We had begged God already for her to be healed. I longed to hold her, to hear her voice. I wanted her home again. Surely the Lord would help by giving me an idea for a way to get her home. Since I wanted her home, wouldn't that be the Lord's desire as well?

I waited in that one spot, curled up on the couch, with long times of silence between my prayers.

"Lord, show me how to pray. What shall I ask for? What do You want?"

I began to hear a voice in my mind, "The mountains will make you well. The mountains will make you well!" It was a phrase that I had read as a little girl from the classic novel *Heidi* by Johanna Spyri. I knew that didn't seem very spiritual, but I just kept hearing it in my head; it seemed to get louder and louder echoing in my soul.

And as if to confirm, I was thumbing through the Psalms and happened upon Psalm 121:1-2, *I lift up my eyes to the hills. From where does my help come? My help comes from the LORD, who made heaven and earth.* (ESV)

Strange as it sounds, this seemed like an answer to me. Peace settled in, and a knowing. Somehow, I knew my daughter would be strengthened and she was going to complete her journey in India.

I kept trying to call her every hour. Eight long hours later, after I had been blanketed with peace and a sureness of what would happen, I finally heard my daughter's voice.

"You will be going on with the mission, won't you?" I asked her eagerly.

"Yes, Momma, I feel stronger now. I can make it."

I did not know the itinerary of the mission trip, but they were soon to go to the Himalaya Mountains. They would be there for ten days. It was during that time that our daughter truly gained her strength. The team walked on mountain trails. Since she was not nearly strong enough to do so, she rode a donkey on the trails instead.

The Lord had answered me with so much peace. He settled me and strengthened my faith. I was able to believe that He would heal her, and she would, at long last, return safely to me. He helped me to release her to Him and to consecrate her once again to His care. What seemed impossible just a few short hours before now seemed like the only option. Not only did I have peace about it and felt sure she would make it home again, but I also wanted her to continue the mission. My desire had completely changed.

God strengthened her as well. Was it because of my time in prayer that she felt a change in the situation? Did my prayers contribute to the Lord helping her feel stronger, giving her courage, and the confidence that she could endure to the end? I feel that they did.

"Why did the Lord call me on the mission trip to India when he knew I would be sick for most of the journey?" she asked me when she returned home.

I quickly replied, "He knew that I needed to learn some things."

There were others who learned many things about prayer and about the Lord during that horrific season of affliction too. Her trip did not turn out the way we had planned it; it was not what we had hoped for. God didn't answer my prayers the way I thought He would when I first started praying. But just the same, a deep, eternal work happened in my soul as a result of the way it turned out.

My Confession: Romans 8:26-27 says, "Likewise the Spirit helps us in our weakness. For we do not know what to pray for as we ought, but the Spirit himself intercedes for us with groanings too deep for words. And he who searches hearts knows what is the mind of the Spirit because the Spirit intercedes for the saints according to the will of God." (ESV) I saw this passage in action when my daughter got typhoid fever.

~ Cheri Bunch ~

14
Be Careful What You Pray For

A friend of mine was very concerned about her son. Because of the closeness of our relationship, her children were almost like my own. I loved them dearly, and they loved me. I have known them since they were babies, and they consider me their second mom.

This particular son of hers seemed to flounder a bit in his young adult years. Unhappy at his work, he started spending more and more time with the wrong crowd. His new friends and his activities while with them were the main sources of my friend's concerns.

My friend had called and emailed me off and on for several weeks with prayer requests for her son. Yet, even with much prayer offered on his behalf, he seemed to be going further and further down the wrong path. Then on a particular Friday, she called me again, making a heartfelt plea for prayers that God would intervene in her son's life. I prayed as she had requested, and I knew she was praying too. I also sent emails to a couple of close praying friends asking them to join us in prayer.

Sunday of that weekend seemed like an ordinary day. My family attended church, as is our normal routine. But Sunday afternoon, I received a strange phone call. The recorded voice on the other end asked for me by name saying that I had a call from the local corrections center, or in other words, the local jail. I yelled for my husband to pick up the other extension. I had never received a call from jail before. I was confused as to why anyone there would know my name or my phone number, and I wanted my husband to be on the line with me.

My husband and I listened as a female voice informed me that someone I knew wanted to speak with me, and she was helping him place the call. Then my friend's son came on the phone, this same young man we had all been praying for. He told me that he had spent the night in jail because his stepfather had not accepted the only phone call he had been allowed to make the night before. He said the nice person who was helping him make this call had told him that he only had five minutes, so he quickly explained that he needed someone to be at the jail at nine o'clock the next morning, which was a Monday, with money to bail him out. He told me that there was nothing anyone could do to get him out until then I assured him that I would try to reach his mother and stepfather, but if I couldn't reach them, either my husband or I would be at the jail in the morning. I promised that he would not be abandoned; someone would be there to post bail for him.

Then I called my friend. She didn't answer her phone, so I left her a carefully worded message. I told her that I'd heard from her son, and I very much needed to talk to her about it as soon as possible. A few hours later, my friend called me back. As I explained what I knew about the situation, she began to softly cry.

71

She told me that she had been at church all morning and afternoon and that was why he had not been able to reach her. She said she was going to make some phone calls to his friends and see what else she could find out. And she assured me she and her husband would be at the jail on Monday morning to post his bail.

A few days later, she called me back with this report. On Saturday night, her son and some of his friends had attempted to visit a club. This club had certain days when they did not serve alcohol and would allow people under the legal drinking age of twenty-one to attend. Actually, her son was twenty-one, but some of the others in his group were not. They thought this was one of the nights when the club would admit them all, but it was not. Her son decided to enter anyway, something he should have been allowed to do because he was of legal age. However, the man at the door didn't think he was old enough and accused him of being underage. He argued belligerently that he was not underage and flipped out his license in an impertinent manner as proof. Because he was so belligerent or "talking trash" as my friend put it, the man at the door ran a check on the license.

The check revealed an unpaid parking ticket and the man chose to call the police, who hauled him off to jail for it. He tried to use his one phone call to reach his mother and have bail posted, but her line had a block against collect calls, so his stepfather was not able to hear anything on the other end and hung up the phone. My friend's son could hear his stepfather and thought he had refused to take the call. Because all of this happened on a Saturday night, the young man ended up spending two nights in jail over an unpaid parking ticket. Since he no longer lived at home, his parents had no idea that anything was awry.

My children have always said they were caught every time

they attempted to get away with misbehavior of any kind because I pray that they will be caught. Some years later, I told my youngest child this story when he was a teen. I told him that when parents pray, their children better be on their guard because God is a God who hears prayers. The children of praying parents will be caught every time. And God will use it for their good, as he did this incident in the life of my friend's son. That was the only time this young man was ever in jail. Today he is a hard-working husband and veteran who saw action in Afghanistan. God pulled him from his rebellion and set him on a path that glorifies Him ... and He used a weekend in jail along the way to do it.

My Confession: At times God's work seems strange and alien. "For the Lord will rise up ... he will be roused; to do his deed—strange is his deed! and to work his work—alien is his work!" Isaiah 28:21 (ESV)

~ Harriet E. Michael ~

15
God Has Given Me A Child!

Over thirty-five years ago, my physician-father delivered an out-of-wedlock baby to a teenage mother. By the time this baby was born, my parents were no longer on the mission field in Africa. Rather, they lived in a small town in West Virginia where my father had a medical practice. The baby he delivered was to be adopted, but things did not go as expected.

When the baby made her entrance into the world, it was evident that she was bi-racial rather than Caucasian, as the adoptive parents had expected. Sadly, the adoptive parents changed their minds about adopting her. She was a perfectly normal, completely healthy, and absolutely beautiful baby girl, but was not wanted by these would-be parents ... or seemingly anyone else in that small West Virginia town in the early 1980s. She had no home to go to, no loving touch of a mother's hands, no strong safe arms of a father to hold her.

My parents told our family that there was a baby who needed a Christian home. I remember it well because my husband and I considered adopting her. She was born about one month ahead of our first child. I was quite pregnant at the time and had made plans for only one baby—one crib, one car seat, one high chair, etc. My husband and I decided we would wait a few weeks to see if a childless couple might want her. But if this baby had no home, we would take her and treasure her.

My parents took the baby home from the hospital. Their home was her home for the first few days of her life. My father's arms were the strong, safe arms that held her. My mother's hands were the gentle hands that cradled her and fed her a bottle in the middle of the night when she cried out in hunger.

My parents had her for about a week and still, no adoptive parents had come forward, until one morning when an interesting thing happened. My father had several surgeries on his schedule that morning. Working in the operating room that day was an African-American nurse my dad had known for many years. Her husband served as a pastor of a small church in town. Dad knew she was a kind woman and a committed Christian.

On a whim, or more accurately, with the nudging of the Holy Spirit, Daddy asked this nurse if she might be interested in adopting this one-week-old baby girl. The woman had not heard about the baby girl and did not even know of her birth. She appeared overjoyed when he explained the situation.

She told him, "My husband and I have been married for fifteen years and in all that time we have never used birth control. We have only one child. He is an eight-year-old boy. Ever since he was born, I have been asking God for another child. A few years after my son was born, God gave us a little girl, but she died from leukemia as a preschooler. I was broken-hearted at that time, but I felt God assuring me that He would give me another little baby girl—another daughter. For many years, I prayed and waited eagerly for that baby, but God did not give her to me. I was beginning to think I had not heard Him correctly, that maybe He was not ever going to give me that little girl I wanted so badly. After all, I am too old to have another child now." She added, "Yes. I want this baby, but I need to call my husband and talk to him about it first."

About an hour later, the nurse came back to my father and told him her husband told her to get their baby girl today.

My father gave the ecstatic nurse the name of the lawyer who was handling the adoption.

The woman and her husband gave this baby girl a home. They couldn't have loved her any more if they had conceived her themselves. They taught her about Jesus. And the little girl grew up to become a beautiful young woman. She had a gifted singing voice—the voice of an angel. She made high marks in school, too. She felt as though my parents were like another set of grandparents to her. Her mom brought her to visit my parents often. And for their part, my parents kept her picture on their refrigerator right beside their other grandchildren.

My father delivered many, many babies in his years as a physician. Every birth is a miracle and every new life is an example of God's creative power—even all the normal births that happen routinely, without any complications. Nevertheless, sometimes a second special miracle accompanies the birth of a child.

My Confession: 2 Peter 3:8-9a tell us, "But do not forget this one thing, dear friends: With the Lord a day is like a thousand years, and a thousand years are like a day. The Lord is not slow in keeping

his promise, as some understand slowness ..."
(NIV) Sometimes when it feels like God is not
answering our prayers, He is really just telling us
to be patient.

~ Harriet E. Michael ~

16
God's Strength in My Weakness

Scripture reminds us that doubting God is never to our benefit. In fact, in Romans 9:20, it compares us to a clay pot doubting its maker. It says ... *But, my friend, I ask, "Who do you think you are to question God? Does the clay have the right to ask the potter why he shaped it the way he did?"* (CEV) Nevertheless, even Christians often doubt Him, like Doubting Thomas, a disciple who followed Christ.

Some years ago, a man came into my life who turned out to be far more of a curse than a blessing. He was a close acquaintance before I began to follow Jesus, and I tried to show the same mercy God had granted me by keeping him as a friend after I became a Christian. However, it's not easy to continue in any type of congenial relationship with someone who continually chooses sin as their go-to lifestyle.

I had prayed often about the situation and was becoming weary. Eventually, I asked God to keep him out of my life completely if he were just going to keep hurting me. Well, I guess

I didn't hear God say, "Crystal, that's your job." So, when he reappeared in my life sometime later with the offering of a seemingly genuine apology, I mistook it as a sign that God was letting him back in. I tried to believe that all my prayers, mercy, and patience were finally bringing me what I had always wanted. I trusted God and even proclaimed my good news as an act of faith.

I should have known better, and sure enough, he hurt me again. This time, he hurt me worse than any backstabbing friend I had ever known. I got home from work to discover he had stolen the $850 my mom and I had put away to pay our rent. To top it off, he'd left town.

My first thoughts were consumed with anger at why God *let* him back into my life. Then came the doubts as to if—and how—God could fix this situation. With that great amount of a cash loss, I could not imagine how He would help me pay my utility bills, let alone my rent. I stomped around with tears flowing from my eyes and frustrated words flowing from my lips. I even told God that He'd let me down and that I would never be able to fix things.

That night, I forced myself to pray before I went to bed, but it was agonizing. I dropped to my knees in front of the couch, and I flopped the rest of me onto a cushion where I proceeded to bury my face. I mumbled a bit and then tried to come up with something that resembled a real prayer. The only prayer I could muster up went something like ...

"God, I know I'm angry with You and I shouldn't be. I really doubt You are even listening to me right now because I know my attitude is not right. I can't even feel Your presence right now. But, just in case You are listening, here is my request: Since I know I can't say the right words, please place my burden on someone else's heart who will be able to touch Your throne for me."

After that, I got up from my pseudo-prayer position and promptly resumed moping and doubting. Now, however, to my list of doubts and anxieties, I added one more—I didn't think a prayer like mine could or would ever reach God's throne … or His heart.

The next day, I spent my working hours watching the clock for breaks and quitting time. That was not my normal work behavior, but I could not put my heart into any tasks that day, and I couldn't wait for three o'clock, my last break before the workday ended. Just as the big hand moved to the number twelve to show me that my break time had indeed arrived, something in me changed. I felt a rush of comforting peace pour over me like warm oil. I had goosebumps and an indescribable feeling of comfort. I asked myself if—just maybe—there could be someone praying for me as I had requested of God? But doubt quickly dismissed that thought as impossible, and I finished my break and went back to my desk.

The last hours of the day seemed easier than the beginning of the day, and the walk home was definitely better than the walk to work had been. When I got home at about five-thirty PM, my mother was on the phone and was crying. I thought, *oh great, now what?* I didn't need anything else to go wrong.

Mom was talking with Peggy, a woman who had started attending our church within the last three weeks. Mom's tears worried me, but I didn't know if I needed to be worried for her or for Peggy. Then, telling me Peggy wanted to talk to me, she handed me the phone. I didn't get much past saying *hello* before Peggy started pouring her heart out to me.

"Crystal, I have no idea what's going on in your life," Peggy said, "but I want you to know that I woke up this morning with a burden for you, and I prayed for you all day. And guess what? At about three o'clock, I touched the throne of God for you."

I believe my knees buckled just from those first words. From a prayer I was sure God wasn't listening to, Peggy repeated—nearly word for word—my two key requests. She said she had a burden for me, and she said that she touched the throne of God for me. She prayed until she felt His presence and got an answer, and I know that it was no coincidence that she received her answer *at the exact moment* I had felt peace fall over me. God even made me a clock-watcher for that day just because He knew what I would encounter when I arrived home that night. He truly is near us in our infirmities.

As we cried together, God healed my heart and forgave my doubts and fears. Not surprisingly, He also made a way for me and my mom to take care of our bills. I trusted His answers, and yet I also wondered (and still wonder):

• How did a woman who had only been at our church for a few weeks, and knew nothing about my situation, know to pray for me?

• How did she know exactly what to pray for?

• Why did she leave the church and become impossible to reach just a few weeks after this incident?

My Confession: I now believe God put her there for the express purpose of letting me know just how much He cared for me. I won't even be surprised if I get to heaven and find out she was an angel on assignment. God knew it wasn't His job to make everything right in my life, but He also knew that, in my humanity, I would mess up occasionally. He even knew I would sometimes doubt Him. But,

God was (and is) wonderfully merciful. He has kept this precious event real to me for well over twenty years now, and He reminds me of it whenever new doubts arise.

~ Crystal A. Murray ~

~ Desperate Prayers ~

Then they cried out to the LORD in their trouble, and he
brought them out of their distress. He stilled the storm to
a whisper; the waves of the sea were hushed.
Psalm 107:28-29 (NIV)

17
Lord, Save My Baby!

Nife had to live. She had survived the birth, but would she continue to live? I begged God for the life of my child.

I saw a good child when I looked at my child. I saw a Moses or an Abraham; a Sarah or a Deborah. I knew my child had a special role to play in this wonderful world. But would God let my baby girl live?

The circumstances surrounding her birth had been overwhelming. I was in and out of the hospital throughout her pregnancy. One day I realized I had not felt her kick for close to 24 hours. The doctors could not hear her heartbeat either. But just before the 24 hours was up, another ultrasound picked up her pumping heart.

Praise God, she was alive. He had answered my prayers.

Even so, I feared either she or I would die with the pregnancy. I prayed earnestly, asking God to spare us. God used family to save my life and the life of Nife. With their help, my baby and I made it through to birth. But right away, it was apparent that Nife was sick. She had an infection, and I was told she either needed to stay in the hospital for seven days or come in two times every day for antibiotic shots.

I was tired of the hospital. After all, I had practically lived there for the previous three months. So, I chose to take Nife home and return with her twice daily, even though neither my husband nor I had a car. Thank God for family. One of my siblings took up the challenge, and twice a day for seven days we drove about forty minutes to get Nife the needed shots for her survival. And my whole family stayed in continuous prayer for the tiny baby God had given me. Nife made it. By God's power, she survived. I now see her growing daily and becoming what God created her to be.

The chapter of 1 Samuel 7 tells the story of how God helped the men of Israel as they fought against the Philistines. In verse 12 we read of Samuel setting up a memorial stone which he named "Ebenezer" as he declared, *Thus far the Lord has helped us.* (NIV) That is how I felt at the time. I still had a child to raise, so my work was far from done, but surely the Lord had heard my prayers and had helped me thus far. Much of God's help came to me through my family.

God created family for love. Family is about loving one another and seeking the good of the next person. God created family so we can have a shoulder to lean on and get help at our deepest moments.

When Nife was about eighteen months old, she fell from my bed and had a swollen place on her head. When the doctor asked for a brain scan, I was scared. I could not go for the scan because of the fear of the unknown. I stayed home and cried out to God, again, for the life of my child. And also, again, I thanked God for my family. My father drove my husband, mother, and Nife for the scan. I was scared and fearful, but my parents were there encouraging me, strengthening me. Nife was their grandchild; they loved her, too, and prayed for her as well. God was gracious to us again, and there was no brain damage of any kind.

Praying for my baby girl was natural for me, and it is also a biblical instruction. We are instructed to pray for others—our family, friends, acquaintances, and even our enemies. God wants His children to commune with Him in prayer. He is never tired of hearing us. We can talk to Him about anything that burdens us. He cares. Pray with family and take time to pray with friends too. Prayer not only helps the need at hand, it also builds better relationships.

Are you part of a family? The answer to that is yes if you are a believer in Jesus since all believers are part of God's family. And as a family, we are to lift each other up with the earnestness that I had when my precious baby's life was at stake. Ecclesiastes 4:9-12 puts it well. *Two are better than one, because they have a good reward for their toil. For if they fall, one will lift up his fellow. But woe to him who is alone when he falls and has not another to lift him up! Again, if two lie together, they keep warm, but how can one keep warm alone? And though a man might prevail against one who is alone, two will withstand him—a threefold cord is not quickly broken.* (ESV)

These verses speak of lifting another up if he or she has fallen. One way to lift others up is through prayer. 1 Timothy 2:1 says this in so many words when it says, … *supplications, prayers, intercessions, and thanksgivings be made for all people.* (ESV)

My Confession: Because of prayer and the love and support of my family, my daughter is alive and well today. Having been the recipient of others' prayers, I find myself now eagerly seeking opportunities to offer my prayers on behalf of others.

~ Tope Omoniyi ~

18
Cast Your Cares on Him

When my parents were serving in Nigeria, toward the end of their time there, a civil war known as the Biafran War broke out. I was born in the Niger River Delta, part of what was known at that time as the "Eastern Region." This part of Nigeria lies in the tropical rainforest and has jungles with monkeys swinging in the trees, crocodiles, and even elephants. This is also the part that tried to secede from the rest of the nation and become "Biafra." By the time the war broke out, my family no longer lived in the Eastern Region. Rather, we resided in western Nigeria in a town called Ogbomoso. This part of Nigeria was spared the worst of the fighting, and for the most part, our days were peaceful in spite of the war.

Even so, tensions, in general, were high all over Nigeria. Tribal infighting, which had always been a problem, was at a peak. At one point during this time, a rumor circulated around my town that there was to be a takeover of the local government. Rumor had it that the King of Ogbomoso was to be killed and his body dragged up and down the main road of the town.

The mission had two sections with the residences behind the large buildings of the hospital and seminary. Those large facilities created a protective barrier between all the houses and the unrest that might have been occurring in the town.

All, that is, except for my home. We lived on the main road into town right next to the seminary.

The rumors of the coming riot concerned my father deeply. If the stories proved to be true, then the king's dead body would be dragged right in front of our home, and we children might be close enough to see such an awful thing. There could be an angry mob accompanying the riot that might see our house and try to pillage or burn it. In my father's mind, his own family, his wife, son, and three little girls might also be harmed. So, Daddy decided it was best to move the family to the home of another missionary on the hospital compound whose house was safely behind the hospital. That compound seemed a little safer than the seminary because the hospital had been built with a stone wall around it to keep people from breaking in to steal the drugs that were kept there.

That was the plan, but much uncertainty remained. My parents didn't know how long our stay would be. We might be with this other family overnight, or if our house was burned down, we might find ourselves living with them for a very long time. My parents didn't know how much to pack or what to do with the belongings that they were leaving in the house. They decided to hide as much as they could. They had brought their wedding silver with them to Nigeria. (And yes, as a child in the heart of Africa, I ate every meal with sterling silver utensils—mine was an unusual existence.) They buried it in the backyard.

During all the busy activities of that day, my older sister did not show the least bit of stress or anxiety. She was about nine-years-old at the time. She was a beautiful little girl with long, dark-brown hair, and eyes as blue as the ocean. She sang and whistled as she followed my dad's orders. Occasionally, she would stop her singing long enough to twirl around and dance a little. Her complete lack of concern frustrated my father. He felt like his world might be coming to an end, yet she persisted in singing. Finally, he questioned her in a sharp voice, "Alisa, how can you sing and whistle? Don't you realize the grave danger we are in?"

Alisa looked up at him with her big blue eyes and replied in her childlike way, "But Daddy. I heard you preach last Sunday and you said to cast all our cares on Him because He cares for us." My dad was completely convicted by her words. He realized in that instance that the one with the inappropriate response to the situation was he, not her.

As it turned out, there *was* a riot in my town that night. The king's dead body *was* dragged down the street in front of my house, but we were safely in the home of another missionary. I can remember hearing that it happened, but I did not see it. My family and I had found shelter in the storm. Our house was not harmed, and the next day we moved back in safely.

My Confession: Sometimes I doubt God and even try to make excuses for Him, and sometimes I am surprised by His faithfulness.
~ Harriet E. Michael ~

19
Terrible Is My Name

"Terrible!" answered the enraged intruder to my father when he asked, "What's your name?"

It was November of 1963, a typical warm, dark night during the early dry season in Ogbomoso, Nigeria. My mother had gone out to visit other missionaries that night and was just returning in the car. My father was home, reading in the living room. My younger brother, sister and I were already asleep in our bedrooms.

Suddenly, without any warning, a Nigerian man yanked opened the screen door and stood in the opening. Holding a knife in his right hand and a broken Sprite bottle in his left, the intruder demanded money from my father and threatened to kill him if he did not comply. Although greatly startled, my father calmly got up from the couch and asked his name.

The intruder lunged toward my father, threatening him with a knife. The look in his eyes showed that he was not in a normal state of mind—perhaps on some type of drug. My father remained composed and told the man he had no money, and then with a firm voice cautioned him to be quiet so as not to awaken his sleeping children. (This specific response would later become the talk of the mission and beyond; how my father's priority when he faced a life-threatening situation was to avoid waking the children.) The man, obviously confused and perplexed at the response of my father, didn't notice that Dad was slowly approaching him, coming closer and closer, until he grabbed and slammed the heavy wooden door into the man who was standing just inside the doorway. The glass window in the door shattered when it hit the man's outstretched arm, and he fled quickly, but without dropping the knife or bottle.

In the meantime, my mother had parked the car just a few yards away when Dad started shouting to her "Stay, stay," meaning don't come this way, stay there. Mom thought he was saying "Snake, snake" and feared that a snake had entered the house, perhaps even slithering into bed with one of the children. (Snakes were known to find their way into the houses.) She had a flashlight and thinking nothing of her potential danger, she kept walking toward the front porch. At this point, my father was frantically worried since he didn't know in what direction Terrible had fled and did not want my mother to have to encounter him. As it turned out, Terrible had run in another direction, and Mom was never in any danger of facing him.

The breaking glass and Dad's yelling had awakened me, but I didn't get up and must have dozed off again. Awakening a little while later, I came out of the bedroom when my parents were sweeping up the glass. They told me everything was okay and to go back to bed. Evidently, they didn't want me to worry about what had happened and have problems sleeping. I never thought anything was wrong and soon fell back to sleep.

When I woke up the next morning, everyone was excited and

talking about what had taken place. I learned about more exciting events that had happened during the night. Another missionary just three houses down was robbed and ransacked during the night. The missionaries were gone at the time and the thief (thought to have been Terrible) was able to get in through the back door of the house.

The next morning, after the police had been through the home, they allowed us to go in, but we were told not to touch anything. I can still visualize the inside of the house. It was a huge mess. Nothing was left undisturbed. Drawers pulled out, clothes, furniture, kitchen utensils—everything scattered about. But one unusual detail has stuck in my mind all these years: thieves did not disturb a small matchbox that one of the missionary kids had been using as a "piggy bank". I guess the thieves never thought that money would be hiding in a matchbox.

Soon after the crime, we learned that Terrible was a murderer who had escaped from prison. A few days later, we heard yelling in the streets of the nearby town. The yelling was similar to the sounds one might hear at a ball game when the crowd reacts excitedly to a great play. As it turned out, the crowd was reacting to the news that Terrible had finally been captured, cut hand and all, but not before stabbing and wounding a policeman. I can remember visiting the policeman at the Ogbomoso Baptist hospital, where my father was the pharmacist.

It didn't take long for the news to spread throughout the town about the white missionary man who had stood up to Terrible, unafraid, and had chased him away. My father's action that night made him a hero to the local people, who referred to him as "John Wayne." However, my father never thought of himself as a hero by any means; after all, he was simply doing what any parent would do … trying to let sleeping children sleep. His care to prevent the awakening of his children, despite the danger he faced as he "stared down" a crazed, threatening murderer, has been discussed and laughed about for years—and happily continues even to this very day. A short time later, all the windows on the mission houses were outfitted with expanded metal to prevent anyone from getting in from the outside, and they remain there today.

That same day, we learned about the assassination of President John F. Kennedy. I can recall seeing the headlines "Kennedy Assassinated" on a newspaper tucked in the satchel of a policeman's motorcycle parked outside the house that was robbed. Whenever someone asks me, "Where were you when Kennedy was shot?" I always have an interesting story to tell.

My Confession: Matthew 6:8 tells us that God knows what we need even before we ask Him. My father did not have time to pray when Terrible suddenly burst into our house, endangering our lives. But God knew my father and my family's needs even without my dad's asking. I thank God for keeping us safe that night.

~ Ron Wasson ~

20
Cat Scratch Fever

Tommy was a typical, happy-go-lucky twelve-year-old boy who played outdoors with friends. A lake in the subdivision offered many opportunities for Tommy and his friends to explore. He was particularly proud of his first-degree senior black belt and was beginning to work on his second-degree black belt in Tae Kwon Do.

In December, Tommy began complaining of mild blurred vision. His RN mom, Cindy, attributed it to several previous head injuries that still caused him some problems. Cindy told him if his vision didn't clear in a few days, she would take him to the doctor.

Tommy, one of his best friends, and Cindy were part of the cast in their church's Christmas program when Tommy told his mom that all he could see was the bright spotlights shining on the stage. Nurse Cindy began asking questions to determine what was happening. She asked if he saw the same thing with both eyes. He told her that it was just his right eye. She told Tommy to close his left eye and tell her what he saw.

"Nothing," he said.

"I'll call the doctor in the morning," Cindy replied, trying to remain calm.

First thing the next morning, Cindy called the eye doctor and told him that Tommy couldn't see out of his right eye. The doctor wanted to see him right away. Thus began a very long road, particularly over the next eight weeks as the doctors performed an exhaustive battery of tests, some repeated numerous times, trying to determine what was causing the blindness.

Cindy and Bill prayed urgently and shared their concerns with their church family who also prayed, even holding special prayer services for Tommy. Although she was a basket case inwardly, Cindy knew that outwardly she needed to be calm and cool like nurses are taught to be, especially for her son. If Tommy had seen her going to pieces Tommy might think there was no hope for him. Thankfully, because of everyone's love, encouragement and prayers, Cindy began feeling a sense of God's peace.

They put Tommy in the hospital for two weeks where they continued the testing, placing him on IV steroids to bring down the inflammation around and at the back of his eye. They sent his blood off to numerous labs in different parts of the country to see if their examination and study would give them an answer to why he had no vision in his right eye. During this same time, Bill was recovering from a recent knee surgery.

After a couple of weeks, the labs began coming back. The doctor told Cindy he wasn't seeing anything out of the ordinary in any of the reports. Cindy looked over all the results with her keen nurse's eye, and she didn't see anything unusual either.

Bill and Cindy discussed whether they needed to take Tommy to a specialist outside of Birmingham, in hopes they could figure out what was going on. But Tommy didn't want to go anywhere; he wanted to stay in Birmingham. He told his parents, "Mom, I know if anybody can find out what is wrong, y'all can." So, they stayed in Birmingham and continued working with the doctor in attempts to uncover the elusive cause of the blindness.

In the meantime, the steroids were taking their toll on Tommy. His demeanor changed. No longer that happy-go-lucky boy, he became depressed and withdrawn. This was exacerbated by having to quit practicing Tae Kwon Do. The meds also changed his looks; his face was moon-shaped.

Tommy was also experiencing horrible headaches. Longing to help her son, Cindy asked God to take the headaches away from her child and give them to her instead. But, if that wasn't possible, she asked the Lord to make all of this bearable for Tommy.

Eight weeks after first visiting the doctor's office, they finally found the answer. Tommy had cat scratch fever, a bacterial infection people contract from infected cats. It is surprisingly common. It is spread from a bite or scratch from an infected cat, or from an infected cat's saliva getting into an open wound or whites of the eyes. In addition to the other symptoms, one possible complication is that the bacteria travels to the eye, causing inflammation to the optic nerve and retina.

The doctor told Cindy about seeing it during World War II, when soldiers were in wet trenches for days on end and not able to change into dry socks and shoes.

After a good bit of scouting around the neighborhood, Cindy and Bill discovered what they believed was the only possible way Tommy could have contracted the fever. Around the lake in the subdivision where Tommy and his friend played, there was a darkened area of dirt they concluded was contaminated. The boys would have walked through it many times.

All the doctors said Tommy would never be able to see out of that eye again because of the damage to his optic nerve, and he would not be able to do anything very dangerous for the rest of his life. Tommy just laughed at the doctors and told them, "I'm not going to quit doing things. I'm an active young man and can't just sit around for any reason." His parents told him to do what he felt he needed to do.

Those eight weeks of not knowing what was going on kept them and everyone else on their toes trying to figure it out. And, they implored all—including family members, the church family, and friends— to pray earnestly and consistently.

For several years, Tommy had no vision at all in his right eye. Then he slowly began to gain some of his vision back. Now, twenty-three years later, he serves as a Police Chief and has total vision in that eye, with the exception of a small spot in the very center.

The doctors were, and still are, baffled. They do not understand how he can see. One doctor said, "His optic nerve was like a stick on the ground—no life at all. How is this possible?"

Of course, Cindy and Bill knew why Tommy could now see. They were able to tell the doctor how they, their church family, and countless others had been praying for Tommy ever since the ordeal began. God had healed his optic nerve.

How was Cindy able to walk through this terrible time in her son's life? She prayed, and the Lord gave her the strength she needed to help her son walk through this with a positive attitude.

During this time, Cindy would think about Romans 8:28: *And we know that in all things God works for the good of those who love him, who have been called according to his purpose.* (NIV)

She also held onto John 3:16, *For God so loved the world that He gave His only begotten son, that whosoever believeth in Him should not perish but have everlasting life.* (NKJV) All she could think of at times was, "because I know my son is a Christian, if he dies as a result of this, I know where he will spend eternity." She gained great comfort as she read 1 and 2 Corinthians and 1 and 2 Timothy over and over. And in the midst of this struggle, she learned to practice Psalm 46:10a: Be still and know that I am God. (NIV)

> *My Confession: I am grateful that I have learned that in every situation, whether it appears positive or negative, it is important to be still and know that God is God. He is our source of strength.*
>
> ~ Cindy Graham ~
> as told to Shirley Crowder

~ Prayers from the Valley ~

Yea, though I walk through the valley of the shadow of death, I will fear no evil; For You are with me; Your rod and Your staff, they comfort me. Psalm 23: 4 (NKJV)

21
Why Lord, Why?

I moved to West Virginia in middle school. Football was huge. Every boy wanted to play football, and every girl wanted to be a cheerleader. I was no exception. I worked hard, learning how to cheer. Our school had two cheerleading squads—varsity and junior varsity. I made neither the first two years I tried.

I remember sitting in the gym during the spring of seventh grade as the next year's cheerleaders were announced, but my name was not called. Karen, a girl from my class, made the varsity squad. I didn't know her well, but we all knew *of* her. Her older sister was a high school cheerleader who had just been crowned *West Virginia's Junior Miss*. Sitting on bleachers, the sun streaming through the small gym windows, my seventh-grade heart thought there could be nothing grander than to be a cheerleader and rub shoulders with people like Karen.

I worked harder than ever, and when names were called the next year, I heard mine.

As our captain, Karen ran a tight ship. In one of our cheers, we spelled out the word falcons, our team mascot, with each cheerleader saying a letter. The day we learned that cheer, Karen kept moving us around in different spots. Each time we performed it, she'd shake her head and move us again. After a while, she stopped cheering and just sat on the bleachers watching us perform and moving us around over and over.

Her apparent need for perfection bugged me. "What's your problem?" I demanded

"You," she calmly replied. "You're my problem. You have the worst southern accent I've ever heard. I had trouble finding a letter you could say by yourself. You don't say 'F-A-L-C-O-N-S'. You say, 'ayef– aya – ayal – C – aowa – ayen – ayas'!"

She was right about my accent. My parents are from the Carolinas, and I grew up among Southern Baptist missionaries, many of whom had accents far worse than mine. She put me on "C".

By sophomore year, we'd become close friends. We weren't allowed to try out for either of the high school squads until we were juniors, so we spent that year traveling to all the ball games, studying the cheerleaders, trying to learn all we could while dreaming big dreams of days to come.

We often hitched rides to games in other cities with some friends of my parents. We'd ride in the back of their station wagon in one of those seats that faced backward. It felt like we were in our own little world. The couple probably overheard every word we said, but at the time, it seemed like there was no one else in the entire world, just Karen and me.

Karen had a crush on Joey, the sophomore quarterback, and I had a crush on Donnie, the sophomore running back. We had it all planned; we'd both make the varsity cheerleading squad our junior year and by senior year, she'd be captain and I'd be co-captain. She'd be dating Joey, I'd be dating Donnie, and our football team would win the state championship. That was the plan, anyway.

Things didn't turn out exactly as we'd hoped—but almost. Karen began dating Joey that winter and Donnie asked me out in the spring. But Joey and Karen broke up within a few months and Donnie and I had a relationship that never quite got off the ground. We sort of half-dated off-and-on for years. Karen and I did make the varsity squad our junior year, however, and by our senior year, she was captain and I co-captain. And we *did* have a state championship football team our senior year with Joey as quarterback and Donnie as the star running back.

After our team won the West Virginia AAA state championship, our school held a large assembly. As captains of the cheerleaders and football team, Karen and Donnie spoke. Both thanked God for the victory.

Toward the end of our senior year, Karen began dating a new guy from a nearby high school. College days came, and we went our separate ways, keeping in touch during school breaks. Our spring breaks overlapped by only a weekend, so we had no time to spend together, but we spoke on the phone, making plans to get together in the summer.

That was the last time I ever spoke with Karen.

On May 29, 1978, I was packing to come home from college when I received a phone call from my father. He said in a soft voice, "Hey Sweetie, do you remember Karen?"

In that instant, I knew something awful must have happened. I assumed Karen had been in a wreck. As I braced for that news, I hoped that she was still alive.

My father continued, "Well honey, she and her boyfriend were

102

murdered last night."

Murdered last night? Had my father really uttered those words? Nothing could have prepared me for that.

"Their bodies were found along with his truck in a remote area," my Dad continued. "They were both shot and his body and truck were doused in gasoline and set on fire. Karen was found face-down in a creek a little way away … honey, I am planning on coming to get you tomorrow, but I could come tonight if you need me to."

I managed to tell him I could wait until the next day. I went back to my room and told my roommate who'd been friends with Karen, too. About that time, a reporter from our town's newspaper called on the hall phone asking to interview us, but I declined.

As my roommate spoke to reporters and then her parents, I closed the door, opened my Bible, sat on my bed, and cried out, "Why, Lord, why?" Through tears, I reminded God what a servant of His Karen had been, and how she'd taken a stand for Him. I was a little angry with God, but more than that, I simply didn't understand.

I don't remember how God spoke to me in those moments, but somehow, I came away with some distinct impressions. I knew I would never get an answer to my *why?* I would *never* understand it in this lifetime.

I also realized God didn't owe me an explanation. The God of the universe did not have to explain Himself to me. But what He had given me was the blessing of having known Karen. Of all the people He could have given that to, He'd given it to me. I also realized that Karen's life had not been in vain. My life would forever be affected by my friendship with her.

Although I would never understand why God had allowed her

to be taken from this world at such a young age in such a horrible way, these truths remained; God was still on His throne, and Karen's life had been ordained by God for His purposes. I knew that for certain because touching my life was one of those purposes.

After arriving home, Donnie called and asked if I wanted to go with him to the funeral home. He said, "When I heard the news, I thought of you, and I just thought you might not want to be alone there tonight." I hadn't spoken to Donnie in nearly a year, but it was nice to hear his voice on the other end of the phone. It was nice to have a friend at a time like that.

> ***My Confession:*** *The God of the universe does not have to explain things to me.*
> ~ Harriet E. Michael ~

22

I Can Still See, Hear, Smell, And Taste

There are just a handful of memories in my life in which I can still see, hear, smell, and taste all the things that happened around me as the event unfolded. That Saturday night is one of them. I was at a hotel in Nashville, attending a teen girls' missions conference where I was to lead a seminar.

Late that Saturday afternoon, as I was riding the elevator down to meet the other speakers for supper, I suddenly had an overwhelming sense that something was wrong and that I needed to talk with my mom and dad. Since this was in the days before cell phones, I went back up to my room and called home but got no answer. That wasn't unusual, but it did add to my sense of foreboding.

I sat on my bed and prayed that whatever was going on with my family, the Lord would intervene and give us strength to walk through it, and godly wisdom and sanctified common sense to make decisions. And I prayed that He would enable me to walk, trusting Him to focus upon the tasks He had laid before me to accomplish during the conference.

I went to supper and shared with the group that I had a sense of urgency to pray for my family, and they joined me in praying. I tried several more times to reach Mom or Dad at home throughout the evening. And although my restlessness grew with each unanswered call, I became more and more aware of the presence and strength of the Lord.

Late that evening, I was in my room when the phone rang. It was my mom's brother, Uncle Bill who lived in Nashville, calling me from the lobby of my hotel. He asked me to come down to the lobby. When I heard Uncle Bill's voice, I knew that my sense of urgency to pray had been the hand of the Lord.

As I made the trip down in the elevator, countless questions flooded my mind: Why was he here? How did he know where I was? These questions were accompanied by a keen sense that something horrible had happened—someone had died.

I sat on the sofa, stunned and in disbelief, trying to process what Uncle Bill was saying as he told what had happened to my brother, Paul. "A train hit Paul and Lil Tim. Lil Tim, dead. Paul, seriously injured, will not live. Chas, cuts and bruises, but he will be all right."

I can still see the tears trickling down my uncle's face as he gently and lovingly answered my question, "Are you sure you got this right? This is impossible." I remember the scent of my uncle's cologne and the strength of his arms as he hugged me tightly. I remember hearing his gentle whispers, "It's okay. I love you. You're okay."

Chicago's "You're the Inspiration" played in the background. I remember the sweet scent of roses in an arrangement nearby and the taste of the salty tears I was crying as I saw and heard groups of people talking animatedly.

Everyone was so thoughtful as they helped care for me that night. I went up to my room and called the ER waiting room to speak with my family. Paul had sustained serious injuries, including a catastrophic brain injury, yet, at that time, his heartbeat was still very strong. My nephew, Lil Tim, died instantly. When the phone rang several hours later, I did not want to answer because I knew it was my daddy calling to tell me that my big brother had also taken his last breath here on earth.

I remember a friend hugging me tightly as I sat on the edge of the bed crying, trying to make sense of it all. I remember talking to God as various Scripture passages ran through my mind, mingling with thoughts of disbelief, prayers, and yes, even anger.

Me: "God, I can't do this."

God: *My grace is sufficient for you, for my strength is made perfect in weakness.* 2 Corinthians 12:9 (NKJV)

I had a very long and restless night. Early the next morning, I went to my apartment to pack. It took a while, but I finally gathered everything I needed and began the trip from Nashville to Gadsden. Although the drive was very familiar to me, this time it was much-dreaded.

I did not want to face the reality of my brother's and nephew's deaths, and I did not want to be alone with my thoughts and emotions.

But guess what? I WAS NOT ALONE.

I sang hymns, prayed, and poured my heart out to my Heavenly Father.

That day, I experienced in full *the peace of God, which surpasses all understanding,* [that] *will guard your hearts and minds through Christ Jesus.* Philippians 4:6-7 (NKJV)

There have been a few other events in my life—before and after Paul and Lil Tim's deaths—in which I can still see, hear, smell and taste all the things happening around me as an event unfolded. The constant in each of these events? The indwelling presence of the Holy Spirit.

Jesus says in John 14:26-27, *But the Helper, the Holy Spirit, whom the Father will send in My name, He will teach you all things, and bring to your remembrance all things that I said to you. Peace I leave with you, My peace I give to you; not as the world gives do I give to you. Let not your heart be troubled, neither let it be afraid.* (NKJV)

What do you do when your world is turned upside down? Someone has said, "When your world is badly shaken, begin with what you know to be true and build from there."

What do I know to be true? Something my friend, Dr. Bryan Chapell, said comes to mind, that the first theology lesson we all probably learned is: "Jesus loves me, this I know, for the Bible tells me so."

In the midst of these world-turned-upside-down moments, did I—and do I now—know that to be true? Absolutely.

What did I remember next?

We love Him because He first loved us. I John 4:19 (NKJV) And then, *But God shows his love for us in that while we were still sinners, Christ died for us.* Romans 5:8 (ESV) And, *The Lord is my strength and my shield; in him my heart trusts, and I am helped* ... Psalm 28:7a (ESV)

How do we have the strength to carry on when things seem unbearable and totally out of our control? We must come to a saving knowledge of our Lord and Savior Jesus Christ (Romans 10:12-13).

Christ-followers are to be totally immersed in the Word of God which bears fruit that is the result of obeying that Word (Psalm 1).

The Holy Spirit illuminates the Word of God in the hearts and minds of non-Christ-followers to bring them into relationship with Christ. The hearts and minds of Christ-followers are illuminated so they understand the Word of God, and are strengthened and comforted by His presence within them (2 Corinthians 4:1-6).

Isaiah 46:4 is a reminder of God's love and protection, and, it has continually helped rekindle my hope in the midst of difficult situations.

> *My Confession: What is my confession? What did I learn? I learned that truly "God is our refuge and strength, A very present help in trouble." Psalm 46:1 (NKJV)*
>
> ~ Shirley Crowder ~

23
I Choose Thankfulness

I've read through the Bible every year since 2003. In my first year of doing this, I came across a verse that radically changed my life—Lamentations 3:39, which says, *Why should any living mortal or any man offer up complaint in view of his sins?* (NASB)

From that day forward, I looked at my life through different eyes. Realizing that everything I had, everything I'd been through, everything that would come in my life, was a gift from God, I began to choose thankfulness as a way of life.

In 2014, I received a serious, aggressive cancer diagnosis. I immediately bowed my head and said, "Father, thank You for this cancer. Please help me to glorify You in it." After so many years of practicing thankfulness, this seemed like the most natural thing to do.

The appointment given to me was three weeks away, so my husband and I prayed and asked God to direct us to another doctor who could see me sooner. God brought to our minds various commercials we had seen about the Cancer Treatment Centers of

America. We called them, and they could see me as soon as I could get there. We thanked God for His provision and started packing.

By the time we arrived in Philadelphia and walked into our hotel that evening, I was starving. When I gave my name at the desk, the smiling clerk pulled out a beautiful leather briefcase from under the counter and handed it to me. "This is a gift for you from CTCA. It gives the contact information, services available, and has lots of room for you to put business cards, papers and anything the doctors give you. There's a hospitality room on the second floor that is expressly for CTCA guests, and tonight is our patient appreciation dinner, starting in half an hour."

Wow. God granted me my request for dinner plus things that I never thought to request.

At dinner, people greeted us and introduced themselves. We met eight people who were also from Ohio. They ministered to us, telling their stories and explaining how wonderful everyone at CTCA was. We sat together at dinner and enjoyed a meal that was as good as a wedding feast.

As we finished dinner, a man went to a microphone at the front of the room. He introduced himself as CTCA's head chaplain and explained that, while they usually offered Bingo as their after-dinner program, this night was different. They'd invited pastors from all over to come see how the pastoral care served the patients at their hospital and to learn how to minister to cancer patients in their home churches. He then asked if anyone in the room would care to share their experience with cancer. My husband raised his hand and was handed the microphone. He told how terrified he was when he found I had cancer. He'd cried for days in fear of losing me and was desperately in need of comfort and reassurance.

With that, people from all over the room stood up, walked

over to our table, laid hands on us, and prayed over us. God had ministered to us again in such a tangible way.

When it was time to go to CTCA and walk through two days' worth of appointments, we asked God to grant us and the doctors great wisdom since we had no idea what it might entail. Throughout the day, I sensed His presence in every circumstance—whether a scan, blood test, x-ray, or physical exam—in all of these things, God provided caring, knowledgeable people who patiently answered every question we had.

On the second day, when it was time for the doctor to show us the results of all my tests and scans, we asked God to make it clear to us how to proceed. My oncologist showed the CT scan, telling us how serious it was, and explained what he would do if we decided to work with him. When he finished giving us all the information we had asked for, he folded his hands, leaned forward, looked me straight in the eye and said, "What do you want to do?"

"I would like you to take it out," I replied. "How soon can you do it?"

"I already reserved the OR for Wednesday morning," he said with a smile.

Once again, God had gone before us, paving the way and making what we needed to do clear to us. We were so thankful.

We prayed before calling our loved ones, asking God to comfort their hearts and reassure them that we were in the best possible hands. Everyone, even our daughter, responded positively, receiving the news with soberness but choosing to trust in God's sovereign hand over my life. I went to bed that night with a thankful heart, feeling completely at peace.

I'd never undergone surgery before, so I was a bit nervous. I asked the Lord to go before me, pave my way, and guide the doctors, nurses, anesthesiologists, technicians, etc. The kind people at CTCA did everything possible to put me at ease, explaining what was going to happen to me, assuring me that my oncologist was the very best in the entire hospital, smiling at me, hugging me, and even praying with me.

In the operating room, one of the doctors asked what my favorite kind of music was. When I said I was a Christian and loved worship music, he quickly turned the radio dial to a Christian music station. The anesthesiologist asked if I preferred mountains, water, or wide-open plains. I said I loved being near a quiet lake with trees all around, and he said, "Okay, think about that now. You're sitting beside a beautiful lake on a quiet, peaceful morning. The water is gently lapping against the beach, the sun is shining, the breeze is blowing through the trees, the birds are singing ...."

I fell asleep with those peaceful thoughts, and the next thing I knew, the surgery was finished. I had also prayed for God to provide someone to sit with my husband to comfort and reassure him during my surgery. God sent two chaplains to the waiting room, and a dear friend who lived nearby came and sat with Fred too. God truly cared for both of us through this entire day, for which we were so thankful.

After we got home, our biological family and church family brought us meals, cards, flowers, blankets, and other things to lift our spirits. My pastors came to pray with me and also sing songs. My recovery seemed swift and relatively painless. They continued to care for me through chemotherapy and radiation. The Lord answered their prayers by giving me strength, keeping me from illness, and allowing me opportunities to share my faith. My church family began holding worship and prayer nights on my behalf. We all ate, fellowshipped, sang songs, took communion, and prayed together. The elders laid hands on me, anointed me with oil, and asked the Lord to heal me and protect me from any further cancer. And now, years later, I remain cancer free.

I don't know what God has in store, but He has shown me the power of prayer, the joy of my salvation, the wondrous love of my church family, and the benefits of maintaining a truly thankful heart. God is so good, and I am so thankful.

My Confession: In everything, give thanks, for this is God's will for you in Christ Jesus. I Thessalonians 5:18 (NASB)
~ Lauri Bucci ~

24
Donnie

The portrait I painted of Donnie and me together still dominates my mother's living room. We're sitting, arms around each other, smiling at everyone who walks in Mom's front door. I don't think Mom would have liked the style had it been of anyone besides Donnie, but it looks exactly like him, so Mom loves it. I never realized until I painted us both, that I am his female double—same green eyes, sandy hair, nose, bushy eyebrows, and the same smile. Maybe God ran out of molds after He made five of us, so he just made me, number six, the female version of my brother Donnie.

And we all sang together. When I was about twelve, I learned to sing the alto lines, so we started a family quartet with Dad and my two teenage brothers switching off between bass, tenor, and the lead while I sang alto. We started at our tiny church, but then other churches invited us to sing.

Then, in October 1979, Donnie was getting married. I was sixteen and would finally be a bridesmaid. I had the fabric for the dress. I was planning to be beautiful in it. There was a box of wedding invitations waiting to be addressed, and Donnie had given Julie a ring.

Then one day, Mom and Dad told us Donnie had a rare form of lung cancer. The wedding was postponed indefinitely. I went to the basement and raged against God. We were a faithful family. No one had ever smoked or done anything to bring on lung cancer. Why us? Why Donnie? I cried, argued, and pleaded as I folded laundry. I have no idea why I folded laundry—it was the kind of thing we did. We just pushed through.

If ever I were going to lose my faith, it would've been then. But even then, though I may have doubted the goodness of God, I believed that there was nowhere else to turn.

My parents knew from the beginning that Donnie was terminal. I'm not sure when they told me, but I didn't accept it. Reality kind of slowly oozed into my consciousness as I watched him lose his hair and his extra padding. We were not a family that believed in the "name it, claim it" religious philosophy of bossing God around, but some of my older siblings decided it was a good time to try. They named and claimed Donnie's healing with all the faith they could muster. In the end they were just broken-hearted, along with the rest of us.

By Christmas, Donnie had lost all his hair and replaced his fiancée with a new girlfriend. I never understood that, but who am I to judge my brother, who must have been suffering incredible anguish? Even with no hair and no meat left on him, the young women couldn't resist him. In spite of everything, he knew how to have fun.

Today it's fashionable for a man to be bald, but back then we all had big hair and lots of it, so Donnie got a wig. That Christmas,

Donnie put his wig on our two-year-old nephew. We all laughed as the little fella ran around in Donnie's big wig. It was all great until Donnie started babbling nonsense and vomiting in that crowded living room.

That's where the road turned with his illness, and none of us ever found our way back again. At that moment, we knew it would be our last Christmas with Donnie. The cancer had spread to his brain.

After Christmas, Donnie went back to the hospital and didn't come home again. My mother, who'd always been home, was now always at the hospital. It became my job to make supper and take care of my little brother, Timmy. I quit cheerleading and just did what I was told. I felt left out and torn. I wanted to see Donnie, but I didn't like seeing him suffer. I knew Mom needed me to care for Timmy.

Donnie was the fourth child of seven, right in the middle of us. We were all close to him, and we all loved him deeply. It seemed like everyone was at the hospital all the time except for me and Timmy. During that time, if I began to feel sorry for myself, it led to overwhelming guilt. I'll never forget the time I tried to make a joke about doing all the cooking myself, saying, "I haven't had a decent meal in ages."

Mom reprimanded, "How dare you complain when your brother is suffering in the hospital with cancer?"

That's the only time I remember Mom scolding me during the ordeal. Had I been the one watching my beautiful twenty-year-old child being wrecked by cancer, I probably would've cursed everything and everyone. Mom and Dad were amazing, somehow holding it together. We didn't say much. There were no words. It isn't fair or right or just for innocent people to suffer so.

That desolate January was finally coming to an end, and so was my brother.

"Suzy, you need to come to the hospital to say goodbye," my parents told me one morning in early February.

It's the only hospital visit I remember. I think each of us felt we should read something from the Bible, so I chose to read Romans 8.

... neither death nor life, neither angels nor demons, neither the present nor the future, nor any powers, neither height nor depth, nor anything else in all creation, will be able to separate us from the love of God that is in Christ Jesus our Lord. Romans 8:38-39 (NIV)

The funeral was almost like an out of body experience. I felt as though I were watching myself. It was a little awkward having both the fiancée and the girlfriend in attendance, but we just smiled, and even sang—I think it was "I'll Fly Away" and "Just a Little Talk with Jesus."

No, I don't mean the congregation sang songs in the service. My family sang spontaneously, a cappella, in four-part harmony as we followed the casket out the doors of the funeral home. I guess it seemed bizarre to the people at the funeral, but it was our way of comforting ourselves, and Mom seemed to need it. Dad probably wasn't able to sing, though.

My father had a smooth, beautiful tenor voice. He led singing at the Church of Christ, and even today the memory of his dreamy voice singing the old hymns calms my spirit. After Donnie died, for years, Dad just couldn't sing anymore.

There was no big announcement that "The Bradshaw Quartet" would no longer be singing; it just happened. People seemed to know it was over for a while. Then, slowly, with the passing of the years, like a long, cold winter finally giving way to spring, Dad began to sing again, and the family with him. No, "The Bradshaw Quartet" was never again an item, but we did sing again with Dad as a family. We sang together at church and on holidays, and some of us, even to this day, sing at an occasional funeral when asked.

My Confession: Sometimes God leads us through the valley. Sometimes the pain feels almost unbearable. But God is in the valley with us. And in time, all is well for those who are in Christ. God didn't heal Donnie like we had hoped, but Donnie was healed just the same, in God's time. God makes everything beautiful in His time. Ecclesiastes 3:11

~ Susan E. Brooks ~

25
God's Grace in Answered Prayer

June 22, 2015, was the day my mom had her second stroke. After much testing and evaluation in the emergency room, they put her on a ventilator and admitted her to the hospital, taking her to the second floor—the heart floor.

The days that followed seemed to drag on at times. At one point, they took her off the ventilator but replaced it when she still did not breathe well enough on her own. Her doctor informed us that he would not try to resuscitate her if she coded. When I heard this, everything in me cried out, "No. We can't just let Mom die!" I remember praying and asking God to heal my mom. I told Him "God, you know my mom. She is a fighter and she will get better. Please help her." God answered those prayers, and Mom survived at the point when the doctor thought she would not.

A few weeks later, the first of July, my mom did not respond when I spoke to her. I could not get her to wake up. I prayed, my family prayed, friends prayed. I even stopped people I didn't know in the hallway of the hospital and in the parking lot, or whenever I passed someone just about anywhere, and asked them to pray for her, too. I went to a ministry website and printed a list of healing prayers to pray over her, and my brother joined me. We held hands and prayed these healing prayers standing next to our mom's hospital bed.

I think it was the very next day when her doctor told me yet again that my mom would not make it. He said he didn't think she would last more than a day. I was told I needed to call a funeral home and make arrangements for my mother's funeral. I felt so bleak inside. I truly believed that God would heal her. Sometimes, I felt I was the only one really believing that God would bring her through this and give her a little more time with those of us who loved her.

I went to an empty room down the hall from Mom to call the funeral home. I sat down and prayed again ... and then placed the call. But while I was speaking with the funeral home making arrangements for burial, a call from my brother came through on my phone. I told the funeral home I would call them back, hung up and quickly returned my brother's call. I couldn't believe my ears when he told me, "Mom opened her eyes." I rushed to her room and held her close. Mom squeezed our hands and responded to us. After that, she continued to improve a little each day, so much so, in fact, that later that month they planned to remove the ventilator.

However, once again, we were warned that she might not survive off the ventilator. My mom was cognizant and knew the doctor thought she might not survive without the ventilator. I asked her if she wanted her family doctor to remove it. She nodded, "Yes."

I screamed to myself, "I'm not giving up. I'm still praying for a miracle." Her doctor removed her ventilator and we waited to see how she would respond. I learned later that they thought Mom would not last the night.

Mom did last through the night and about five days later was transferred to a rehab center. My mom's doctor said he had to tear up the rulebook where Mom was concerned. She certainly did not follow the normal rules of how stroke victims usually respond and progress. He said everything was in God's hands. Mom continued to improve and was able to talk better. In August, we gave her a luau party, and she was even able to go outside for it.

In the next couple of months, Mom bounced back and forth between the hospital and rehab. In November, the Lord called my mom home.

Though God eventually took my mom home to heaven, He nonetheless answered my prayers concerning her, too. He allowed my family to have several more months on earth with our beloved mother. And He graciously allowed her some good days in that extended time where she felt well enough to enjoy her family and friends and even have a luau party.

God was faithful to answer Mom's prayer, too. When she prayed, asking Him to forgive her sins and become her Savior and Lord, He did just that and gave her the grace, mercy, and strength she needed to live a life that honored Him. And when God called her home in November, He answered all of our prayers. She is now perfectly healed and lives forever in His presence.

My Confession: I learned firsthand the truth of a saying I have heard most of my life: God is good all the time and all the time God is good.
~ Debbie Lynn Wells ~

~ *God's Mysterious Ways* ~

Oh, the depth of the riches of the wisdom and knowledge
of God! How unsearchable
his judgments, and his paths beyond tracing out!
Romans 11:33 (NIV)

26
A Visit to The Witchdoctor

The summer of 2000, I served as a mission coach with college-age interns, researching what it would take to plant churches among a large Muslim tribe. As part of our research, small groups of the team spent a week living with different members of the tribe. Amanda, one of the interns, and I were guests of a certain family.

My host often sent me out with his cousin, Susan, who was keeping Amanda. She took us out to learn different aspects of tribal life. Her youngest cousin, Hattie, a recent high school graduate, tagged along. We visited farms, orchards, a blacksmith shop, and a little market.

One morning, Susan excitedly told us that we were meeting an old friend of hers named Frank who she said was a charlatan. A charlatan? I was confused. Why would she be so proud to know him but call him a charlatan?

Maybe I had misunderstood Susan. What she said sounded like the English and the French word charlatan, but perhaps it was a tribal word that meant something completely different. A similar thing had happened a few weeks earlier when I thought the people were talking about a canary instead of a cooking pot.

After walking several miles, we arrived at Frank's hut. He did not speak French, so we communicated through Susan, who spoke both French and the native language. I still wasn't sure what a charlatan did and asked if he could show us.

Frank brought out a set of small conch shells, similar to necklaces people buy as souvenirs. "Oh, you're a jewelry maker," I said. "I'll get gifts for my mother and sister."

Susan laughed and shook her head. Frank didn't make jewelry. Still confused as to what Frank did as a charlatan, I asked for a demonstration.

Frank invited me to come inside his hut and sit on the dirt floor. Frank spoke his language. Susan translated into French for me, and then I translated into English for Amanda. Frank rolled the little shells out on the dirt floor in front of us.

Oh cool. An African game. He must make toys. I decided I'd learn the game, so I could teach it in VBS back in America.

Frank said something in the tribal language, Susan translated into French and I into English. "Hattie, you are headed to college."

He must have noticed how anxious Hattie was since she was waiting to hear if her test scores were good enough to get into college.

As I translated for Amanda, I noticed out of the corner of my eye that Frank had picked up the shells to roll them again. I refocused on the game, so I could learn the rules.

Frank rolled the shells a second time. He studied the shells and said, "Amanda's first child will be a girl." I translated this into English.

Okay, one of these shells was Amanda. One was her baby. Oh,

125

this game was like one my sister had ... wait a minute.

Suddenly, it dawned on me who Frank really was.

This was no kid's game. He was telling fortunes and practicing magic. He was not a toymaker at all—he was a witch doctor. Charlatan meant witch doctor. I was the coach of a team of missionary interns, and I was having spells cast over them.

My heart cried out to God. *Lord God! I have been a complete idiot and need Your protection over me, Amanda, Susan, and Hattie and against any demon or evil spirit attached to Frank. Please work through this horrible situation despite my mistakes.*

Now it was Susan's turn to have her fortune told. Frank threw the shells and studied them again. "Susan, someday you will marry."

Oh, Frank. You are such a fake. These predictions could apply to anyone. Of course, Hattie would go to college. There's always a fifty/fifty chance of any first child being a girl. Susan had a steady government job and wanted to marry. Of course, she would marry someday.

Now, it was time for my fortune. Frank scooped up the shells and threw them out like dice. He studied a moment, then shook his head with a blank look on his face. He picked up the shells, rolled them out again, scratched his head, looked at the shells inquisitively, and rolled them out a third time. Finally, he asked if I spent a lot of time with pastors or something. Susan, who was translating, didn't know I was a missionary. She thought I was a teacher with a group of students studying African culture. I said my father was a preacher and I volunteered in church at home.

Frank explained that the spirits could not see anything for me because they could not see through the bright cloud around me. God had heard my prayer. He was there with us.

Despite my embarrassment at being lost in translation, God had shown up and proceeded to work through my mistakes. With Susan translating, I spent the morning talking with Frank about his life as a witch doctor. He spoke of being an apprentice to an older witch doctor and years spent learning to open up to the spirits. I asked how he could be a Muslim and a witchdoctor.

Frank claimed to be a good Muslim since he still practiced all the things Mohammed required. He explained that Allah was far away and he could not be bothered with people's everyday problems. Frank said he tried to work with spirits here on earth to persuade them to help people through their problems.

What a totally warped picture of God. Frank did not know that God loved him. I explained that I was a follower of Jesus Christ. I told him that God cares for us, knows when a sparrow falls to the ground and even knows the number of hairs on our head. We can pray to God for help when we are sick or in need, much the same way a child asks his or her father for help. God has that kind of love and concern for the people He has created.

God took my translation mistake to later open up even more conversations with Susan and Hattie about trusting God and praying to Him. Even though I would never have planned to have magic practiced over my mission interns, God used my error to give us an opportunity to openly share the gospel with Frank, Susan, and Hattie.

I would like to say that Frank, Susan, and all the rest are Christians now, but I honestly don't know. A civil war closed off access to the area for several years. Missionaries were evacuated, but an African pastor friend visited the area several years later. The one church in town had shrunk to a handful of members as Christians from other tribes had fled when civil war broke out.

That handful of Christians decided that it was up to them, and they felt they had nothing to lose in sharing their faith with the Muslims around them. They began evangelizing everyone they knew. That one little church of less than five people went on to start over forty churches in and around the town where Frank, Susan, and Hattie lived. I am still praying and trusting God that they are among the new believers.

My Confession: Prayer works even when we make huge mistakes. Even in our ignorant attempts, God is able to bring good and great things about.

~ Anonymous ~

27
Treasures from Heaven

My son, Robert, was so excited to get his high school class ring. He brought home the information with all the various options and asked if he could please order one. Of course, my husband and I said yes, even though it would be costly. We had bought a school ring for his older brother, so yes, Robert would get one, too.

He pored over the options, designed his ring, and ordered it. At the Junior ring ceremony that November, dressed in coat and tie, he proudly walked up when his name was called and received the treasured box containing his ring.

Five short months later, we took a family trip to my sister's house in South Carolina over spring break. My sister lived on ten acres of land. Much of it was wooded and it had a pond. During the week we visited, Robert and his cousin of the same age were all over those ten acres, and they fished in the pond from the pier.

The day of our departure for home, Robert could not find his treasured class ring. We all looked everywhere—inside my sister's house, in her yard, on the pier, and in the car. Robert and his cousin walked around the ten acres for an hour staring at the ground, but to no avail. His ring did not turn up anywhere.

My husband and I didn't even scold him for losing his costly ring because it was obvious he felt bad enough already. A sad teenager rode in the back seat of our car on that long drive home.

Robert went back to school that Monday with no ring on his right hand. In the afternoon when he got home from school, he asked me to call his aunt and see if they had, by chance, found his ring. Sadly, my sister reported that though they were all still on the lookout, the ring had not been located yet. She assured me that if anyone in her family found it, she would notify us immediately.

A couple of days later, the ring still remained lost. That day, Robert decided to do his homework outside. It was a sunny, spring day, so he took his backpack to a table, which sat on a concrete patio a few steps from our back door.

A few minutes later, he came running inside the house.

"Mom, Mom!" he shouted.

I stopped what I was doing and ran to him, concerned. But the minute I saw his face, I knew that whatever he wanted to tell me was good news, not bad.

"Look, Mom," he said as he held out his cupped hands.

I could not believe my eyes. There, inside his hands, sat his once-lost class ring. I asked him where in the world he'd found it, and he told me this story.

He said he sat down at the patio table to do his homework but was still saddened about having lost his ring. He said for the first time, he actually prayed about it. He leaned back in his chair, looked up toward the sky and said, "God, can You please help me find my class ring?"

Then, he opened his backpack to get his book out to begin

reading the pages he had been assigned for homework. All of a sudden, he heard a ping on the concrete next to his chair, close to his feet. He looked down and there sat his ring, sparkling in the sun. Robert went on to ask, "How did it get there?"

I just shook my head in disbelief.

He continued, "Well, I suppose it could be that the ring was in my backpack all along and when I opened it and reached in to slide my book out, the ring got pushed out. And I guess it's possible that the book pushing against it gave it enough momentum that it continued to slide across the six inches or so to the edge of the table until it fell onto the concrete floor."

"I guess that's what must have happened," I responded.

Robert's eyes twinkled. He said. "That's not what I think happened, Mom. I have looked in my backpack several times and have taken it to and from school for several days now. And I've slid books in and out of it. No, that's not what I think happened."

"Well, what do you think happened, then?" I asked.

With a big grin on his dimpled face, Robert replied, "I think maybe God was just waiting on one of us to pray about it and ask Him for help. And when I finally did, I think God just picked it up off the ground in those woods, or from the bottom of the pond, or someplace like that and then just dropped it down from heaven—right at my feet."

My Confession: God knows what we need before we ask, and sometimes He gives us what we need without our asking. Other times, I think He waits for us to pray before He answers.

~ Harriet E. Michael ~

28
See What God Just Did!

When my friend's son was a sophomore in high school, he found himself at a new school. In the fall of that year, the Homecoming dance at his new school had been in the gymnasium of the high school. So, when the next dance, Winter Ball, rolled around in January, he naturally assumed it would be in the school gym as well. However, it was not. It was in a location several miles away from school. Getting there involved crossing the Ohio River into Indiana. The school must have announced the dance location, and the other students knew it from previous years, but my friend's son somehow did not catch this bit of information until the day of the dance.

He had attended another school in the same town the year before and asked a girl from that other school to be his date. The girl's mother had agreed to let her go to the dance under a certain condition; that the newly licensed young man would not be driving on the interstate that night. The young man assured his date's mother that he did not have to take an interstate to get to school where he thought the dance was to be held. However, unbeknownst to the boy, the drive to the actual location would require interstate travel, since it was to be held away from school.

The day of the dance, the girl's mother learned at work from a co-worker where the dance was to be. Thinking that my friend's son had lied to her, she withdrew her permission for her daughter to go.

The afternoon of the dance, my friend's son left school, stopped by the florist to pick up the corsage for his date, and then came home to get ready. He received a phone call on his cell on the way home from a new friend, inviting him and his date to an after-dance party. These after-dance parties could sometimes be a point of concern for parents, especially in this case, given that my friend and her husband did not know the child who was hosting the party or his parents. Just as her son was petitioning his parents for permission to attend the party, he received another phone call. This one was from his date telling him she was not able to come to the dance with him. She explained that her mother had found out it was across the river in Indiana and would require interstate travel to get there, so she thought he had lied to her.

My friend said it was not a pretty sight at her house. Chaos ensued. After hanging up the phone, the young man began letting his anger out in loud expletives. His father, who was trying to discuss options with him, was growing angry too, and their voices escalated louder and louder. My friend quickly realized that she might just be in the way. She felt she had nothing positive to contribute to the situation, so she retreated to her bedroom and prayed.

After a while, the son, at the coaxing of his father, called his date's mother and managed to explain himself. He apologized for his misunderstanding about where the dance was to be held and explained why he had this misunderstanding. Apparently, he convinced the woman because she agreed for her daughter to go to the dance with him, even though it meant traveling a very short distance on the interstate. But she stipulated he have the girl back by midnight.

This was not completely pleasing to him. He complained to his parents that the dance would not end until midnight. Thus, he would have to leave early, and he would not be able to attend the after-dance party. My friend and her husband explained to him that he had a choice. He could go to the dance alone, in which case he could stay for the whole dance and attend the party afterward, or he could take his date, but he would have to comply with her mother's requests and have her home by midnight. My friend made the suggestion that her son bring his date home to his house by midnight since it was closer to the dance, and they would not have to leave quite as early. She suggested he see if the girl's mother could pick her up from his house at midnight instead of him taking her home. This option is what the young man chose to do.

I still remember my friend telling me about this situation. She added, "So do you see what God just did? God has my son coming back to my house by midnight and I didn't have to make him, and his father didn't have to make him."

My Confession: *God often works in unexpected ways.*

~ Harriet E. Michael ~

29
A Kiss from God

A kiss is not just a kiss. There are many different kinds—that memorable first kiss, friendly pecks on the cheek from old friends we haven't seen for years, wedding kisses, the tender kiss of a new mother holding her baby for the first time. There are goodnight kisses and the first day of school kisses.

Some kisses say, "I'm sorry," or "You're special." Kisses are sometimes given to comfort. In sadness, you have perhaps tearfully bestowed a kiss to say a last earthly goodbye to a loved one. Whatever the reason, kisses all have a voice. They are a precious gift from God, who is Himself love.

A number of years ago, I participated in a Bible study in which the idea of being kissed by God came up for discussion. Did God kiss His children? How would He do so? Several ideas came to our minds—notes, phone calls, hugs, little gifts. I remained quiet, as I had been during most of the previous sessions.

I was living under a cloud that prayer had not lifted. Prayer itself had become difficult. Oh, I knew God was there. After all, isn't He always? He just didn't seem to be saying or doing anything.

Later that week I sat alone in my garden, surrounded by plants, listening to the sounds of water flowing over the rocks in the fishpond. These sounds had always erased the tension of work days, fatigue, anger, or any other invading emotion. That day nothing penetrated the sense of emptiness, of having totally failed both God and those I loved.

Family dynamics were at an explosive level, complicated by the fact that our children were adults, two with spouses. Unlike skinned knees, a bandage and a kiss wouldn't help—and God was silent. Perhaps it would never be fixed. I was a shell, too empty for tears.

In the stillness of late afternoon, a sound caught my attention. More slowly than I'd ever moved, I turned my head toward the sound. Hovering less than three feet from my face was a beautiful emerald green, ruby-throated hummingbird.

Mesmerized, I froze, expecting him to dart away. Instead, he moved closer, stopping about 12 inches from my face. I was eye to eye with a hummingbird. Amazingly, he stayed, wings beating almost too fast for sight. His gaze from those tiny bright eyes seemed to penetrate my own. I remember wondering for a second if he was going to poke my nose—and not caring if he did. I wasn't about to move. I was even careful to breathe as softly and slowly as possible.

Time seemed to stop, though it may have been no more than a minute before he veered off and up, soon lost in the trees. I sat motionless for several minutes, wanting to keep the picture of this exquisite experience in my mind. "Thank You," I finally said. "for allowing me to be in the midst of this miracle."

A little while later, I knew what had happened. Knowing my need, God had responded. I had been kissed by God.

Through the years, God has continued to use the hummingbird as His messenger. I began spending half of each week staying with and caring for my elderly dad, who lived 75 miles away and had several health problems. With an understanding boss, I was able to switch from teaching a five-day preschool class to a two-day class.

The time Daddy and I had together was a lovely gift. We talked, laughed, and fussed occasionally. Most medical appointments and grocery trips ended with time simply driving around, down roads he remembered, sometimes photographing his childhood homes. We grew very close, treasuring each other.

Even so, there were occasional times when trying to be wife, teacher, grandma, Bible study teacher, and daughter/caregiver were blessings almost too heavy to carry. On Monday mornings, before I left to go to Daddy's farm, I went early into my garden.

There I prayed, trying to turn every moment over to God. As tears fell on my devotional book or Bible, I sometimes heard the beating wings of *my* hummingbird. God seemed to whisper "Look, child … I'm here." Shining in the sunlight, the hummingbird would be at the feeder or on the nearby butterfly bush—his favorite spot. His presence always brought a smile, a thank you, and a new supply of strength.

When Daddy died, I gave little thought to the hummingbird until I felt his absence. Fall settled into winter, with many trips to Daddy's farm, taking care of the house and land. The next summer, I realized that the hummingbird had not returned after his winter migration.

Each season fell into the next. I wondered if perhaps the little creature had been assigned to another soul in need. I'd known from the first months of his presence that he was more than a hummingbird. He was a beautiful, tangible reminder of God's strength, enabling me to meet the needs of family, job, church, and to be whatever Daddy needed. The little bird was an affirmation that the Lord would carry me through times I didn't want to face.

My Confession: God's still, small voice can sometimes be beautiful.

~ Victoria Hicks ~

~ *Miraculous Answers* ~

Jesus looked at them and said, "With man this is impossible, but not with God; all things are possible with God." Mark 10:27 (NIV)

30
The Baby Who Would Not Breathe

My father sat at his desk seeing patients at the hospital in Nigeria one day when an orderly came running into his office. The orderly breathlessly explained that he had come from the Maternity Center. Mrs. Ladeji, the midwife matron of the Maternity Center, had sent him to fetch my physician father. "Mrs. Ladeji says you must come quickly," he exclaimed.

Assuming Mrs. Ladeji must be facing some kind of medical emergency, my father jumped up and ran to the delivery room. When he opened the door he found Mrs. Ladeji leaning over a newborn baby who was lying on a delivery table, giving it mouth-to-mouth respirations. She paused long enough to tell him that she had delivered the baby about thirty minutes earlier, but that it would not breathe. She explained that she had been doing mouth-to-mouth all that time.

Giving respirations to an unresponsive person is quite tiring, even if the recipient is a baby. Dad could see right away that Mrs. Ladeji was exhausted from her efforts, so he took over the job. He

140

gave continuous, small puffy breaths into the newborn's mouth, pausing occasionally to see if the child would breathe on its own. But each time he checked, the baby was unresponsive. He checked the heart rate and the beat was around 130 beats per minute, normal. A heart rate of below 100 would've indicated trouble, but as long as someone else breathed for him, the baby survived.

Realizing they could not keep this up indefinitely, Daddy asked for a small syringe with a tiny needle and gave the infant a small dose of Caffeine Sodium Benzoate into the muscle of the thigh. This is a stimulant which he hoped would jar the child into breathing on his own. He and Mrs. Ladeji rubbed the muscle so that his body would pick up the medicine. The baby took an occasional weak breath, but it was not enough. He would have died if left to breathe on his own.

Mrs. Ladeji and my father continued to alternate breathing for the little boy. By this time an hour had passed since his birth and he was still not responding as he should. The two health professionals discussed the situation and concluded that the baby was not adequately picking up the mild respiratory stimulant that had been given. So, in desperation, my dad asked for another small syringe and a tiny long needle through which he administered a small dose of Coramine, a stronger stimulant. This time he plunged the tiny long needle directly into the child's heart. He withdrew blood to be sure he was in the heart and then injected the Coramine. The infant responded with some stronger breaths, but still did not breathe as he should. His handful of shallow breaths were simply not enough to sustain his life.

Dad and Mrs. Ladeji continued resuscitating the tiny life on the table in front of them. After about fifteen more minutes of mouth-to-mouth resuscitations, my father turned to Mrs. Ladeji and said, "I have done all I know to do. I think we need to pray."

The two stopped their resuscitation efforts, and pulled the little bundle onto their laps, stretching him between them. They each touched his little body as they bowed their heads. My father prayed an exhausted and desperate prayer saying, "Lord, I'm at the end of my rope. We have done all we know to do for this baby and still, he does not breathe well. We do not know anything else to do but to turn to You for help. If You want this baby to breathe, You will have to do it."

When they opened their eyes, they saw the baby take its first really good breath. Neither could believe what they saw. His little chest began to rise and fall rhythmically, as it should, and within a just few minutes the newborn was breathing normally. The little guy had no further trouble. Mrs. Ladeji and the midwives watched him very carefully for the next couple of days, but he showed every sign of being a normal, healthy baby boy. They allowed the mother to keep the baby by her side knowing that she would keep a close eye on him, too. After a few days, the mother was able to take him home breathing just like any other baby.

My Confession: So often we turn to God after we have tried everything else on our own. I can't help but wonder if the baby would have responded sooner if my father had only asked God for help sooner.

~ Harriet E. Michael ~

31
Heavenly Operator

Rrring! Rrring! Rrring!

The phone in the kitchen rang as my family walked through our front door, suitcases in hand, after returning from a long trip to visit my dying grandmother, my father's mother. The year was 1964. My missionary family was back in the USA from Nigeria, West Africa, for this one year because it was our furlough year. And it appeared it was also going to be the year my grandmother was going to pass away.

Maa, as I called her, had been sick for quite a while. She had an autoimmune disease called Polyarteritis Nodosa which had kept her wheelchair-bound for some time. I could not remember her when she was not in a wheelchair, but I had seen pictures of her walking with friends. My parents, especially my father, had strongly desired to be with his mother when she passed away. They had made it a matter of prayer and were thankful their furlough, bringing them back to America, happened when it did.

I loved my grandmother. Even though she was wheelchair-bound, I always enjoyed visiting her. She had a small brick ranch home in South Carolina located across from a lake. Her yard was filled with tall pine trees and flowers of all kinds. To this day, the smell of gardenias reminds me of her.

We had visited Maa many times earlier that furlough year. Being at her home and around her delighted me. She always smiled. She read us books, told adventure stories, and laughed with the most contagious laugh. My father told me once of a time Maa laughed at a local zoo near a parrot cage. The parrot mimicked her laughter, which made her laugh even more, and the more she laughed, the more the parrot mimicked. Soon a crowd gathered to hear them, and yes, to laugh at the funny spectacle. This was my cheery grandmother and she kept that sweet disposition to the very end.

As a child, I didn't know how sick she was. She greeted me with open arms, homemade Kool-Aid popsicles, and a warm smile in spite of her illness. She even had the women who cared for her push her wheelchair outside where she played tag with us. As we ran around her wheelchair, she tried to tag us and laughed. I can still remember running around her chair, laughing with her, while the strong smell of fresh pine mingling with the soft scent of roses, camellias, and gardenias wafted my way.

But the recent visit made me realize she was gravely ill. She lay in a hospital room, and I could tell she was not herself. She seemed very weak. In fact, my father explained to my siblings and me that his mother, our beloved Maa, was going to die soon. We stayed for several days, visiting her in the hospital and saying our goodbyes, thinking she was dying. But then she seemed to get better. Since my father needed to get back to work, we went home.

Rrring! Rrring! Rrring!

My father hurried to the phone. "Hello?"

"Hello, sir. This is the operator," said the woman's voice on the other end of the telephone. She continued, "I have finally been able to reach the person you asked me to reach, and I now have them on the phone. One moment and I will connect you."

"What?" My father was completely confused. The operator said she had reached the person *he had asked her to*. He hadn't asked her to reach anyone. He hadn't even been home. In fact, he had been on the road for the past four hours, not to mention this was long before the days of cell phones.

"What? I don't understand."

"Hello?" This was a new voice, but my father recognized it immediately. The voice belonged to his sister, Patty.

"Patty?"

"Oh, Keith. I'm so glad you called. Maa has taken a turn for the worse and is not expected to make it through the night. I wanted to call you, but I knew you were traveling, and I thought you were probably not home yet. I'm so glad you called me."

Hearing the urgency in Aunt Patty's voice, my dad got off the phone quickly and told us we needed to get back in the car and go back to South Carolina to see Maa. And that's exactly what we did. We picked up our unopened suitcases, walked back through our front door, and piled into the car.

My grandmother passed away that night, but we arrived in time for my dad to be with her. My mother took my siblings and me back to Maa's familiar house, where we slept soundly. We were very tired from riding in the car for so many hours. But my dad and his sister were at the hospital, beside the bed of their mother, each holding her hand when the angels came to escort her to Heaven.

How did that phone call happen? My father did not initiate the call and neither did my aunt. The telephone rang at my house and almost simultaneously at my aunt's house. My dad picked up our phone and said hello, and my aunt picked up her phone and said hello, and they were connected. But how? The voice on the phone that connected them identified herself as an operator. According to her, my dad had contacted her and asked her to try to get through on my aunt's phone line—but Daddy never did that. If you ask me, the operator was an angel … or perhaps the man who impersonated my father and placed the call was an angel. Either way, we were blessed to have had an angel intervene and help my father be with his mother and sister at such an important time.

And God miraculously answered my father's prayer to be with his mother when she died.

My Confession: Psalm 116:15 tells us that "Precious in the sight of the Lord is the death of his faithful servants." (NIV) When my grandmother died, God answered my parents' prayers in a way they never would have dreamed.
~ Harriet E. Michael ~

32
Angel Arm

The warm, soothing sun had turned my skin a golden brown. I lay on a lawn chair by a swimming pool, relaxing—my family playing happily nearby—thinking how blessed I was. My chair stretched out by the pool's shallow end so I could keep a close eye on my daughter—the youngest of my bunch. From this vantage point, I could see the length of the pool to the other end where my two older children played with their cousins.

Splash. My middle child, eight-year-old Robert, hit the water again in another backflip. He was having fun. He swam to the edge and hurried up to do yet another backflip. The condo pool where we vacationed didn't have a diving board, so Robert launched his backflips from the edge of the pool at the deep end. He had done this many times, but I could tell as his feet left the ground, this one was different. This time he hadn't been close enough to the edge.

What happened next is forever etched in my memory. I can see it again now as if it were yesterday. It plays in my mind in slow motion. Robert jumped up and flipped his body in midair. But as he came down into the water, the back of his head hit the side of the concrete pool.

Smack. The sound was awful. His head jerked forward and he sank into the pool.

I stood up and screamed, "No." And under my breath, I whispered, "Lord help."

My brother-in-law Teddy saw and heard it too. Before I could even begin to run in Robert's direction, he leapt out of his chair making his way there. Teddy had lounged closer to the deep end anyway, and I froze in fear.

Just as Teddy got to the edge of the pool, Robert's right hand and arm surfaced. He seemed to be floating up in a sitting position with his right arm extended upward, his hand held in a tight fist. Teddy didn't even have to reach down in the water, because by the time Teddy made contact, Robert's hand was above the water. Teddy grabbed that extended arm and pulled Robert safely out of the water.

Blood poured from Robert's head. I suddenly came to life and sprang into action. Grabbing a towel, I wrapped his head and yelled for someone to get my husband as quickly as possible. In a few seconds, John arrived. He picked up Robert in his arms and loaded him in the back seat of our car. I rode in the back seat too, cradling Robert's head in my arms. Robert was awake, alert, and talking, for which I was thankful.

At the Emergency Center, the doctor took X-rays and cleaned and stitched his head wound. He told us Robert's skull had not cracked, so we needed to take him home and watch him carefully for the next forty-eight hours. That's how it all happened. I remember it clearly.

However, Robert told me an entirely different story a few days later.

According to Robert, he felt his head hit against the side of the pool, and then immediate and severe pain. He sank to the bottom. He can vividly remember sitting on the bottom of the pool, opening his eyes underwater and looking up.

That's when he saw the hand. It extended down in the water to get him. He was glad to see it and assumed an adult member of his family had reached in to rescue him. Robert grabbed hold of the hand and felt his body being pulled up to the surface. Since it was his Uncle Teddy who had pulled him out of the water, he assumed Teddy's hand had been holding his all along.

Teddy and I know differently. Teddy never reached his arm down to the bottom of the pool. How could he? A human arm is not long enough to stretch to the bottom of the deep end of a swimming pool. But that's what Robert experienced. He remembers sitting on the bottom of the pool and feeling the concrete below him. And he clearly remembers grabbing hold of an outstretched hand extended to him. Just as he also remembers being pulled up—his body lifted upward without any effort on his part. I, and others, certainly saw him come to the top of the water with his right arm extended and right hand in a fist as if he were holding onto something or someone.

I have only one explanation—God heard my prayer and dispatched an angel to reach a strong arm down into the water and rescue my child.

That was many years ago. Today when summertime rolls around, and I'm enjoying vacations with my now-grown family, when I relax on lawn chairs and with my family enjoying themselves nearby, I can't help but remember that incident. And I know that yes, I am very blessed indeed.

My Confession: God even answers prayers that are quickly uttered in a moment of panic—sometimes in miraculous ways.

~ Harriet Michael ~

33
Struggling in Prayer

Have there been times in your life when you struggled in prayer? I remember such a time in my own life. I woke up in the wee hours of the morning and sat straight up in bed. A loud noise had awakened me. I saw that it was 2:45 AM. Further investigation did not uncover a source for the sound, so I lay back down and closed my eyes. A friend of mine came to my mind. I had a strong sense that she was in some sort of danger, so I began praying the Lord would protect her and lead her to safety.

I got out of bed, turned on the light, grabbed my Bible and began reading and praying. I had no idea what might be happening, but I was certain she needed prayer.

The burden to pray felt so heavy that I was having difficulty breathing. I didn't care if it was 3:18 AM, I was calling my friend. I called her home, but she did not answer. I thought it strange that the answering machine didn't pick up, but it had been acting up lately, so, that didn't necessarily mean something was wrong. However, since I knew her husband was out of the country, I was quite concerned.

The burden was so real and strong that I felt as though an elephant were sitting on my chest. I dressed as quickly as I could, praying aloud over and over, "Lord, lead her to safety." I called one more time before leaving home, to no avail. I grabbed my keys and headed for her house. As I rounded the corner onto her street, my heart almost stopped beating.

A police car sat in her driveway and another in front of her house, but I didn't see her or her car. I pulled to the curb and noticed it was 3:25 AM. Whispering, "Lord, help me." I got out of my car and headed toward the house. Several neighbors saw the flashing lights and had also gathered to see what was going on.

An officer stopped me and said I couldn't go any further. I explained I was a friend of the family and that I was concerned about her not answering her telephone so early in the morning. I also made sure he knew that her husband was out of the country on business.

I found out from one of the neighbors that another neighbor, a surgeon just getting home, saw her leave her house around midnight. He had asked her if she was all right, and she had replied that she was going to check on someone. Then another neighbor thought she saw a man crawl out of my friend's bedroom window around three in the morning, so she called the police.

As soon as I overheard an officer say my name, I stepped up, introduced myself, and asked why the officer had said my name. He informed me that my name and number were on an emergency list by my friend's telephone.

The officer allowed me to come into the house and look around. Drawers were open in the china cabinet. I went to her bedroom and nothing looked disturbed. Next, I went into the den.

I asked if the officers had turned on the lamp by the rocking chair in the den. When they verified the lamp was on when they arrived, I knew she probably had been praying for someone and might very well have gone to the hospital to check on them.

The officer radioed dispatch to contact hospital security and ask them to see if my friend was in the waiting room.

In minutes, the police dispatcher put a call through from hospital security. My friend was indeed there. The security officer told my friend someone had tried to rob her house and that she needed to go home to go through the house with the police officers.

When my friend arrived home, she told the officers and me that earlier that night, the Lord had put on her heart that she needed to pray. She got up and went into the den, turned on the lamp by her rocking chair, and started praying. In a few minutes, the Lord impressed upon her to go to the hospital ICU, so she dressed and went.

With tears of joy pouring down my cheeks, I literally jumped up, clapped for joy, and shouted, "Thank You, Jesus." My friend began praying aloud, "Thank You, Jesus." because although she didn't yet know the whole story, she knew I had been praying.

The confused police officer radioed for the paramedics to come into the house. I think he thought two straitjackets were needed.

I held my friend's hands and prayed aloud, "Thank You, Jesus, that we both listened to You. Amen." I began singing, "To God be the glory." My friend joined me as we sang, "Great things He has done ... and give Him the glory great things He has done."

More officers began gathering in the kitchen. After singing, my friend and I sat down at the kitchen table where we began to piece together the events of the night. I figured that the burglar had probably heard me leave the message, when the answering machine finally picked up, that I was on my way over, so he fled through the bedroom window.

Colossians 1:29 came to mind, so I quoted, *For this I toil, struggling with all his energy that he powerfully works within me.* (ESV)

As we concluded, one of the officers looked at my friend and said, "I think you're both in shock, but you are one lucky lady." He produced a pistol that had apparently been dropped as the burglar had escaped through the window.

Practically in unison, my friend and I said, "Luck had nothing to with it. God did!"

God answered my prayer and led my friend to safety from the burglar with a gun.

> ***My Confession:*** *I have learned to not ignore the Holy Spirit's prompting to pray. When someone comes to mind, or the thought that I need to call or check on someone comes to mind, I act upon it quickly.*
>
> ~ Shirley Crowder ~

✝

~ On the Lighter Side ~

A cheerful heart is good medicine ... Proverbs 17:22a
(NIV)

34
You Asked for It, You Got It!

The desert can seem eerie at night, especially when you're alone. But with a full moon and a friend, there's something peaceful about a summer's drive with the car windows down. Well, it's peaceful unless your friend has a way of attracting trouble and your car seems to have it in for you.

The old 1966 Toyota Crown Deluxe had its share of troubles, but it mostly did its job of getting me from point A to point B as needed. It liked to die at intersections, but since I have short legs and despise clutches, I'd say I was mostly to blame for that trouble. Using the choke to avoid the regular case of intersection hiccups was a tremendous help—until it got stuck. Boy, is it ever scary to see yourself hurtling toward a huge fence and not having the leg strength to press the brakes hard enough to fight the stuck choke button. I screamed and pulled, and the choke popped back in place just in time to put on the brakes before the car went through the fence.

But the choke wasn't the problem with the old car the night of my desert drive. It was a beautiful summer night with a sky full of stars on display like only the desert can do. Kingman, Arizona, is still a small town, but back in the mid-1980s, it had a population of around 10,000 people. The main roads and highways were paved, but even now, there are plenty of dirt roads within the city limits. Though not paved, the dirt and gravel roads are typically graded to keep them from becoming undrivable in the rain, making them smooth enough for a nice country drive.

So, there I was, a young girl in my early twenties who had only recently become saved and baptized in one of the town's small churches. I knew a lot about God and the Bible from childhood Sunday school classes, but this recent confession of faith and dedication to serving the Lord was the most serious of my life. I was convinced I would follow Christ forever from that point. I don't want to give even a hint of glory to the enemy of our souls, but I will say that my decision to become a Christian was quickly followed by a number of "incidents" that made it a struggle to keep walking the new path before me. Though I struggled, I did not quit in spite of what almost happened that night.

The moonlight was so bright that the road seemed lit by street lamps. The old metal signs along the road were clear and readable as well. As we ventured along a twisting dirt path, we came upon a set of train tracks with a large sign proclaiming the property belonged to the railroad. I panicked. I know now that it was referring specifically to the rails, but then I thought it was the road on the other side of the tracks. I decided we should turn around and go the other way rather than cross over and become *trespassers* and risk prosecution. Fear can sure ruin a good evening.

Turning around on a dirt road in the middle of the desert, no matter how brightly lit by the moon, turned out to be a bad idea.

While I backed up, a rear tire ended up over part of the tracks and ground that had crumbled. The weight of the car caused the tire to drop into a crack of the crumbled blacktop and get wedged between it and one of the rails, but the rest of the car was on the track.

We pushed. We pulled. We lifted. We bounced. We did everything we could to dislodge the tire. When nothing would work, we decided to get out the jack, lift up the car, and push it off the jack into the desert. It was better than being on the track. But wouldn't you know, a train was scheduled at that crossing at about 2:30 am., and we could hear it roaring up the track from a couple miles out. There was no time to even get the jack out of the trunk, let alone get the car boosted up and pushed off the jack.

My friend went running down the track, waving his arms like crazy to try and get the train to stop, but the train kept rolling. The engineer sounded the train's horn almost non-stop from the time he noticed someone on the tracks. When I saw that the inevitable crash was about to happen, I ran the opposite direction and fell into the middle of the desert brush while covering my ears, closing my eyes, and screaming at the top of my lungs. While screaming, I was pleading in prayer, "God, get the car off the tracks. Please get the car off the tracks!"

Soon, I felt a hand on my shoulder, and a young man (from the Hualapai Indian reservation we had apparently been driving around on) was asking me what was wrong. I lifted up my head to see the huge flames that now engulfed my car and said, "What do you think is wrong? Look!" I regret now that I was so mean to someone who was obviously trying to help, but I suppose stress mixed with fear can make a person not act very nice. Still, he understood, and he walked me over toward the train that was now gathering quite the collection of firetrucks, ambulances, and police cars. I learned later that the way the crocheted afghan on the front seat burst into flames made the engineer think a person was in the car and caught fire, so he reported the accident as a death. That brought many more people to the accident scene.

A policeman walked me near one of the train cars where the trailer it was hauling was mounted above the flatbed open enough for me to crawl through. On the other side, two ambulance drivers reached out to me with open arms, so I took their invitation and collapsed into them as they half-carried me to the back of the ambulance. Once they figured out I was unharmed except for stress, they tried to give me words of encouragement about "things being okay" and such. I remember crying to someone that I was upset because I prayed that God would get the car off the tracks and He didn't. Then, someone pointed to the car (no longer in flames) and said, "Look, it's off the tracks now." And then they added something like, "Be careful what you pray for, and maybe be more specific next time, and say something like 'Get the car off the tracks *before* the train hits it.'"

> ***My Confession:*** *According to the Proverbs of the ever-wise Solomon, a merry heart does good like a medicine. The funny perspective of my answered prayer was certainly a comic relief that night.*
>
> ~ Crystal A Murray ~

35
Pray for Flying Saucers

"Pray for my cat—she's sick."

"I need you all to pray for my dog, Zoe. She died last week."

"We saw a dog on the road on the way to church. Please, please pray for him."

"My hamster needs prayer."

"Pray for my goldfish. We had to flush him last week."

I am a children's pastor; welcome to my world.

It was Children's Day during morning worship, and the pastor followed his normal routine, asking for prayer requests after he opened the service. The adults did not have a chance to speak, as the children's hands raised like popcorn kernels popping open, each kid with his or her own request. The pastor did not know what to think, as requests were given for nearly every animal in town. I am always shocked when I see roadkill in our area, considering that with the youngsters' pleas, we cover the critters in prayer from week to week.

Over the years, I have learned that children have an innocent view of the world and take God at His word when He says all things are possible with Him. They will not only ask, seek, and knock—they will beat that door down. Nothing is off limits, as they will say any and every sort of thing on their minds and then some.

I first learned about children and prayer not long after I became a Christian twenty years ago. The Sunday school teacher for the primary class had stepped down, and the pastor asked me to fill in temporarily. I have since learned that, in church volunteer language, "fill in temporarily" actually means "until Jesus comes," but I will save that lesson for another day.

That Sunday school class, which served as "boot camp" for my later work, consisted of five to six Kindergarteners on any given week. The regulars were my eldest son, two of his buddies, and seemingly shy twin girls who attended church with their grandmother who accompanied them to class each week to make sure they would stay put. She and I had quite a time with these youngsters, who taught us both a lot about prayer. Sometimes it was hard to keep a straight face.

Once they opened up to me, the twins had the most unique prayer requests, normally around a particular theme that would last for weeks.

"Pray for jellyfish."

This was their first request, recurrent for a long time. No one, not even their grandmother, knew why they wanted to pray for jellyfish, as they had neither been to the beach nor the ocean. Even so, for several weeks, I obliged.

"Lord Jesus, watch over the jellyfish in the sea."

"Father, let the jellyfish keep to themselves and not hurt people who are swimming near them."

From there, they moved on to loftier heights.

"Pray for flying saucers."

This request was the girls' most urgent and long-lasting plea, as we railed heaven about flying saucers for over a month. I have always tried to honor children's prayer needs no matter what, but this one was a challenge. How was I supposed to pray for flying saucers? I finally had a revelation.

"Lord Jesus, please keep the flying saucers up in the sky, close to You and away from us down here."

The young ladies were satisfied, and Jesus answered that prayer, as there were no UFO sightings in the tri-state area during that time.

Another young boy only visited church occasionally, but his request was always the same.

"Pray for my grandfather—he died last year."

I did not want to belittle the boy's grief, and I'm sure he missed his grandpa. That being said, how do you justify such a request? Luckily, after several awkward repeats of the same plea, Jacob, one of my other students, had enough and took matters into his own hands.

"Why do we have to pray for your grandpa? HE'S ALREADY DEAD!"

Jacob was not one for tact, but, I had to admit, he did have a point.

Recently at my church, we began a bus ministry, bringing in several children who did not have a traditional church background. My pastor, a single man, never married, with no kids of his own, had no background in children's ministry. With our latest group, he has had his hands full and has gotten an education with their prayer requests.

For the first few months with these children, their hands would pop up like the aforementioned popcorn, and there were numerous mentions of animals, teachers, long-passed grandparents, little siblings, and more. Each child would have request after request, so prayer time lasted about as long as a regular church service.

The pastor finally came to the realization that we could not spend that much time for this part of the service, so now he asks the children to only raise their hands if they have a request, explaining that the Lord knows their hearts and their desires before they even speak them. So far it is working, but we will see.

I think of the classic hymn "Just a Little Talk with Jesus." Oftentimes, we adults think we should not bother God with the small things in life. Kids know otherwise—they do not mind having a little talk with Him about every little detail of their lives. He truly "sweats the small stuff," and children buy into that.

My Confession: (A prayer warrior who spends much time with young children.) Jesus said, "let the children come to me" Matthew 19:14 (ESV) as He rebuked His followers for shunning the younger set. Who knows? Maybe those disciples were tired of prayer requests about the local donkeys and camels. However, Jesus knew about the miracle of childlike faith. Plus, He definitely has a sense of humor.

~ Carlton W. Hughes ~

36
Out of The Mouths of Babes

Children say the funniest things.

I remember working in the preschool department of my church a few years ago when my number came up on the volunteer list. A little boy, not older than three or four, came up to me and tugged on my shirt. I looked down and said, "Yes?"

He looked up with earnest eyes and said, "You know what I want to be when I grow up?"

"What?" I replied.

With all the sincerity an innocent child can have, he answered, "A humpback whale."

I suppressed laughter as I patted the adorable child on the back and said, "That would be awesome."

When I told a friend about it, his response was equally funny. He said, "And that's why humpback whales have been taken off the endangered species list. They have a great recruitment program."

The prayers children offer can be equally as funny.

Many years ago, when my second son was only three or four years old, our very old dog, Kricket, a toy poodle, died. We had taken her on vacation with us rather than leaving her at a kennel because we knew her passing was imminent. Sure enough, the second day we were there, she died.

About a week later, the family sat around the dinner table about to eat supper. My husband reminded the children to bow their heads for the mealtime prayer and my second son threw his hand up in the air, started waving it, and exclaimed, "Oh, oh! I want to pray sumpun!"

Gaining his dad's permission to pray, the little guy climbed onto his chair and stood straight up while the rest of us remained seated. He folded his hands and said in his little stuttering voice, "D-d-dear G-g-god. P-p-please make Kricket a-a-all better again. Amen."

I worked hard to suppress my giggle as my husband gently thanked our son for his prayer and tried to explain that although God certainly could make the dog (who was buried by this time) all better, He most likely would not, and sometimes we just have to learn to move on when sad things happen. But I must confess, I half expected to see our dead dog come running through the kitchen door, considering the earnestness of this sweet child's prayer.

✝

My parents' church service usually included a children's sermon. The pastor or another staff member would sit down on the top step of the pulpit area, call the children to the front of the sanctuary and have them sit beside and around him while he told them a Bible story.

One year, when my oldest child was quite young, we visited my parents' church where they had such a sermon as a part of their worship. My oldest happily went down the aisle and sat around the associate pastor along with the other children. At the end of the brief children's sermon, the pastor asked if any of the children would like to close their time with a prayer. My son's hand shot up.

Since his was the only hand in the air, the others apparently too afraid to pray out loud in front of the entire church, the associate pastor recognized my son's hand and thanked him for his willingness to pray in "big church." I could feel the pride surge in me at my brave son's eagerness to pray.

We all bowed our heads and my son said in a loud, clear voice, "Dear God, Thank You for the food. Amen."

That pride that had surged in me was replaced quickly by amusement and a little bit of embarrassment. After church, an elderly gentleman, whom I had known for many years, approached and told me how sweet it was that my son had been willing to pray in public. I commented, "Yes, but he prayed for food as if he were at the dinner table."

With a twinkle in his eye, the wise old man smiled and replied, "One can never be too thankful for food, you know."

My sweet grandson's bedtime prayers were delightful when he was little. He prayed lengthy prayers thanking God for just about everyone he knew or had ever known, as well as every pet he had or ever had, along with any pets that family members currently had or ever had too. And he would pray for all of these by name. Then, as he was about to end his prayers, he always added, "And dear God, thank You that we live on land and not hot lava."

That was not a one-time prayer—it was something for which he seemed genuinely thankful during a couple of years of his young life. I don't know what television show or video game made him ever think of having to live on hot lava, but as my daughter would say, "His prayers give me a fresh appreciation for things I might otherwise take for granted. I mean, how awful would it be if we had to live on hot lava!"

> *My Confession: The way a child learns about God, life, and the world around him is no doubt as precious to God as it is to us. And their sweet prayers must likewise be treasured by their loving Heavenly Father.*
>
> ~ Harriet E. Michael ~

37
A Dog's Prayer

December of 2003 was a very hard time for my family. We had some family issues, my teenage daughter had missed a week of school due to a hospitalization and was saddled with a lot of make-up work, and at the same time, my husband had the first of two surgeries. This particular surgery was a total hip replacement, but it was soon to be followed by a total knee replacement a few months later.

My sweet parents drove from South Carolina to Kentucky to spend a few days with us to help me out during this difficult time. They came to watch my elementary-age child, help my daughter get caught up in her studies, and do about anything else that they could to ease my burden, allowing me to spend time at the hospital with my husband.

My mother is no animal lover, but my husband is. We had two dogs at the time, and my husband might have wanted more if I hadn't insisted that three was my limit.

My poor mother spent the few days she was at my house trying to keep my house cleaned, my family's laundry done, and meals for the family cooked so I could be at the hospital with my husband. She also kept the dogs fed, watered, and let outside whenever they needed to go out. One particular day, it had rained the night before, so the backyard was quite saturated. Both of our dogs tracked in mud that day, causing my mom to have to spend extra time working on the floors and carpet to get them clean again. One of the dogs also spent the day eating grass, whenever my mother let him out. This dog always loved to chew on wet grass. Of course, he then proceeded to vomit this partially chewed, wet grass all over the family room carpet. My mother patiently cleaned that up too.

That was the day my husband came home from the hospital, so by late afternoon, we were all home. At dinner time, he felt up to joining us at the table. As we sat around the dining room table preparing to eat the delicious meal my mother had lovingly prepared, we all bowed our heads to ask the Lord's blessing on our food. It has always been my parents' custom to hold hands when they prayed before a meal, so since they were visiting, my family did this as well.

"Let us pray," my father said while bowing his head, closing his eyes, and extending both of his hands out to the persons on his right and on his left. We all bowed our heads, closed our eyes, and reached our hands out for the hand of the person next to us. Then, my father led us in a prayer.

When the prayer ended, my mother, with her hand still stretched out, lifted up her head, looked at my youngest child and asked, "Ty, why is your hand wet?"

"My hand's not wet," he replied. Then, lifting both of his hands out from under the table so that we could all see them, he added, "Grandma, you are not holding my hand."

My mother bent her head back down and looked in the direction of her right hand, which was still outstretched beneath the table. She let out a startled scream and jumped from her seat.

When she finally regained her composure, she told us she had apparently been holding the nose of our dog—the very same dog who had been so much trouble to her all that day.

My six-year-old son, Ty, burst into laughter. He said he had watched it all happen and wondered why his grandmother had chosen to hold the dog's nose instead of his hand.

Apparently, when my mother reached out to hold the hand of my youngest child, this funny dog of ours stuck his nose in my mother's open palm. Ty said he reached his hand out to grab his grandmother's hand but then saw her wrap her hand over the dog's nose instead, so he just put that hand in his pocket and bowed his head.

My mother's perspective was quite different. She reached her hand out after she had already closed her eyes and then felt what she thought was Ty's wet hand. Thinking she had taken hold of her grandson's hand, she just assumed he probably had a good reason for it being wet. He was just a six-year-old, after all. So, she closed her hand around what she thought was the little, wet hand of her sweet grandchild.

The dog sat very obediently and let my mother hold his nose throughout the entire blessing.

To this day, one of the funniest moments of my life was when I realized my mother had held the nose of our dog throughout a dinner-time prayer. Maybe the dog was trying to make up to her for all the trouble he had caused her that day by patiently letting her hold his nose for reasons he probably figured only she knew.

My Confession: I think God has a sense of humor. I think He sometimes looks down and laughs too.

~ Harriet E. Michael ~

Bible Verses about Prayer

Harriet and Shirley would like to share some of their favorite Bible verses that pertain to prayer.

Then I proclaimed a fast there at the river of Ahava, that we might humble ourselves before our God to seek from Him a safe journey for us, our little ones, and all our possessions. For I was ashamed to request from the king troops and horsemen to protect us from the enemy on the way, because we had said to the king, 'The hand of our God is favorably disposed to all those who seek Him, but His power and His anger are against all those who forsake Him.' So we fasted and sought our God concerning this matter, and He listened to our entreaty. Ezra 8:21-23 (NASB)

The LORD restored the fortunes of Job when he prayed for his friends ... Job 42:10a (NASB)

In return for my love they act as my accusers; But I am in prayer. Psalm 109:4 (NASB)

... Now the LORD saw, And it was displeasing in His sight that there was no justice. And He saw that there was no man, And was astonished that there was no one to intercede ... Isaiah 59:15b-16a (NASB)

... You who remind the LORD, take no rest for yourselves; And give Him no rest until He establishes And makes Jerusalem a praise in the earth." Isaiah 62: 6b-7 (NASB)

Call to Me and I will answer you, and I will tell you great and mighty things, which you do not know. Jeremiah 33:3 (NASB)

Arise, cry aloud in the night At the beginning of the night watches; Pour out your heart like water Before the presence of the Lord. Lamentations 2:19a (NASB)

I searched for a man among them who would build up the wall and stand in the gap before Me for the land, so that I would not destroy it; but I found no one. Ezekiel 22:30 (NASB)

... How can you sleep? Get up and call on your God! ... Jonah 1:6a (NIV)

While I was fainting away, I remembered the LORD, And my prayer came to You, Into Your holy temple. Jonah 2:7 (NASB)

'But when you pray, go into your room and shut the door and pray to your Father who is in secret. And your Father who sees in secret will reward you'. Matthew 6:6 (ESV)

... rejoicing in hope, persevering in tribulation, devoted to prayer. Romans 12:12 (NASB)

Devote yourselves to prayer, keeping alert in it with an attitude of thanksgiving ... Colossians 4:2 (NASB)

Epaphras, who is one of your number, a bondslave of Jesus Christ, sends you his greetings, always laboring earnestly for you in his prayers, that you may stand perfect and fully assured in all the will of God. Colossians 4:12 (NASB)

About the Compilers

Harriet E. Michael

Harriet E. Michael was born in Joinkrama, Nigeria, deep in the African Jungle in the Niger River Delta, where her father served as the only missionary doctor at that station. A few years later, the mission moved the family to a larger hospital in Ogbomoso. Co-author, Shirley Crowder and her family lived right across the dirt road. The two children became constant playmates. Today they continue to enjoy their lifelong friendship.

Harriet is a multi-published, award-winning writer and speaker. She has authored or co-authored five books (four nonfiction and one novel) with several more under contract for future release. She is also a prolific freelance writer having penned over 200 articles, devotions, and stories. Her work has appeared in publications by Focus on the Family, David C. Cook, Lifeway, Standard Publishing, *Chicken Soup for the Soul*, *The Upper Room*, Judson Press, Bethany House, and more. When not writing, she loves speaking to women's groups and teaching workshops on freelance writing.

She and her husband of over 38 years have four children and two grandchildren. When not writing, she enjoys substituting at a Christian school near her home, gardening, cooking, and traveling.

Follow her on:
Facebook: https//www.facebook.com/harrietmichaelauthor
Blog: www.harrietemichael.blogspot.com
Amazon: amazon.com/author/harrietemichael

Shirley Crowder

Shirley Crowder was born in a mission guest house under the shade of a mango tree in Nigeria, West Africa, where her parents served as missionaries. She and co-author Harriet E. Michael grew up together on the mission field and have been life-long friends. Shirley is passionate about disciple-making, which is manifested in and through a myriad of ministry opportunities: biblical counseling, teaching Bible studies, writing, and music.

She is a biblical counselor and co-host of "Think on These Things," a Birmingham, Alabama, radio/TV program for women. Shirley is commissioned by and serves on the national Advisory Team for The Addiction Connection, Several of her articles have appeared in "Paper Pulpit" in *The Gadsden Times'* Faith section's, and in a David C. Cook publication. She also has written articles for Life Bible Study and Woman's Missionary Union. She has authored and co-authored several books.

Shirley has spiritual children, grandchildren, and even great-grandchildren serving the Lord in various ministry and secular positions throughout the world.

Follow her on:

Facebook: https://www.facebook.com/shirleycrowder

Twitter: https://twitter.com/ShirleyJCrowder

Blog: www.throughthelensofScripture.com

Amazon: amazon.com/author/shirleycrowder

Contributors

Anonymous is a 7th-grade science teacher who enjoyed working in Africa on a short-term mission trip and hopes to return to the field someday.

Susan E. Brooks, M.Ed., started teaching English in 1987. In 1996, she moved to Mozambique, Africa, with her family, where she taught art and English at an international school. After returning home and teaching in Kentucky high schools for nearly ten years, she then traveled to Turkish Cyprus in 2009, where she taught American Literature and English at Near East University. Susan returned again to Kentucky in 2011 where she currently enjoys painting, drawing, and writing while teaching art at Portland Christian School. Susan has published three children's books and has written another for Baxter's Corner books.

Lauri Bucci is a lifelong resident of Cleveland, Ohio and has been happily married to Fred, also a lifelong Clevelander, for 37 years. God blessed them with two beautiful children, Melissa and Daniel. He also blessed them with a family HVAC business which they ran together for 30 years. They helped co-found Cornerstone Community Church in 1989 and still worship and minister there today. Lauri serves as the music director and also as a certified biblical counselor. Lauri and Fred launched a new ministry, Addictions Victorious, through which they hope to help addicts, their families, and their friends to be transformed to new life and transformation in Jesus Christ. Over the years, Lauri has experienced the loss of her father to a massive heart attack, her twin sister to cancer, her son to drug addiction, plus her own cancer diagnosis and subsequent health issues. But in all of these things, she has chosen to trust God and to be thankful, and this is the message she shares with everyone she meets.

Cheri Bunch grew up in Kansas but currently resides in Kentucky with Scotty, her high school sweetheart and now husband of over 38 years. They have five grown children and six grandchildren. She is a graduate of West Coast Bible College. She currently teaches at a clinic that helps people with reading disabilities. Writing has been her passion since she was a small girl. She always has a story to share, many of them sharing how the Lord has impacted her walk of faith. She especially loves journaling and encourages others to journal. She has written articles and devotions for the Proverbs 31 Ministry and is a member of LCW (Louisville Christian Writers).

Tracy Crump has published more than two dozen anthology stories, including nineteen in *Chicken Soup for the Soul*. Her articles and devotionals have appeared in national magazines such as *Focus on the Family, ParentLife, Mature Living, Upper Room,* and *Quiet Hour.* She has written for a Christian newspaper and was a columnist for *Southern Writers Magazine* for four years. As co-director of Write Life Workshops, Tracy conducts workshops and webinars that encourage others to "Write Better, Write Now!" She is a regular presenter at conferences and presently serves as registrar for the Mid-South Christian Writers Conference in Memphis. She edits *The Write Life,* a popular newsletter with callouts, and her latest endeavor is recording courses for Serious

Writer Academy and conducting presentations on their Serious Writer Tour. But her most important job is Grandma to two completely unspoiled grandchildren. Visit Tracy at:

- www.TracyCrump.com,
- www.WriteLifeWorkshops.com,
- www.SeriousWritersAcademy.com/Tracy-Crump

or on social media at www.Facebook.com/AuthorTracyCrump or www.Twitter.com/TracyCrumpWrite (@TracyCrumpWrite).

Laquita Havens lives in Fairdale, Kentucky. She has been married 52 years to her favorite companion Bruce, and they have three daughters, five grandchildren, and four great-grandchildren. Her favorite hobbies are children, teaching Sunday school, story-telling, puppets, and writing. Laquita is a freelance writer with four published Children's Books, titled, *Opportunity Jesus' Chosen Donkey, Dumber, the Talking Donkey, Sammie's Pajama Party*, and *I Was Made to Love*. She also has two published devotionals co-authored with Dr. Sheila Embry, *Dear Cousin* and *Cousins Too*. Laquita was a puppet director for over thirty years, having many scripts published thru Lifeway and other drama and puppet publications. Now retired from producing puppet productions, she has more time to share Jesus one-on-one with the kids in the neighborhood who visit on her front porch.

Victoria Hicks is a wife, mother, and grandmother. She lives in Louisville, Kentucky with her husband, Gary. Victoria enjoys being with their grandchildren, reading, needlework, and researching ancestors. She has written articles and poetry for her church newsletter, "The Carillon," along with advent and Easter collections. She has written dialogue and co-written lyrics for both youth and adult choir productions and enjoys writing fiction. One of her stories was published in *More Christmas Moments* published by Grace Publishing. She is a graduate of two courses at Institute of Children's Literature, is a member of both Louisville Christian Writers and E-Liners. Active in her church, Victoria teaches the Good Shepherd Bible Study class, sings in the choir, and is a member of Women's Missionary Union.

Carlton W. Hughes is a professor of communication at Southeast Kentucky Community and Technical College and the children's pastor at Lynch Church of God. His writing credits include several devotionals from Worthy Publishing: *The Wonders of Nature, So God Made a Dog, Just Breathe, Let the Earth Rejoice,* and *Everyday Grace for Men.* His work has also been featured in *Chicken Soup for the Soul: The Dating Game* and *Simple Little Words.* He was the ancillary writer for *Inter-Act,* an interpersonal communication textbook. He has won awards for playwriting and for his work in children's ministry. He is on the planning committee for Kentucky Christian Writers Conference and is a contributor to two blogs, almostanauthor.com and inspiredprompt.com. He and his wife Kathy have two sons, Noah and Ethan. Carlton is a fan of chocolate, good books, basketball, and classic television shows like *I Love Lucy.*

Anne Crowder Lucas was born in Birmingham, Alabama, to Jeannie and Ray Crowder. After her parents served in various churches in southern Alabama and the panhandle of Florida, they were appointed by the Southern Baptist Convention as career missionaries to Nigeria.

Anne's family served in several locations in Nigeria. At the age of 9, she went to a mission boarding school in Nigeria. At age 16, the family returned to the United States for Anne to complete high school and acclimate to American culture. In her senior year of high school, she lived in the States with an aunt and uncle while her family returned to Nigeria.

Anne attended Samford University, graduating with a Bachelor of Arts in Psychology. She met the love of her life, David Lucas, while singing with the Baptist Student Union Choir. They were married after graduation. They have two grown children, two daughters-in-law, and three granddaughters. Anne has worked most of her life in various roles including teacher, IT Manager, management consultant with Ernst & Whinney (Young)., and with IBM in consulting, sales and customer service. For the last nine years, Anne has served with e3 Partners Ministry leading the medical and overall e3 mobilization strategies. She serves throughout the world. She and David are active in their church, Liberty Park Baptist in Birmingham, Alabama. Learn more about e3Partners at www.e3partners.org

Crystal A. Murray is a freelance wordsmith and creative mind with a vast array of interests. She enjoys writing haiku & other forms of poetry, and when writing non-fiction, that which is devotional in nature is her favorite style. Crystal most enjoys the works she shares within her community at Louisville Christian Writers, aka LCW, where she has been president for five years and a member for 20+ years. She finds joy in encouraging other writers, including helping them in the critique process and would like to read every item written by every member of her group. "But," she says of herself, "I'm often torn between my many creative drives. Should I read? Write? Take pictures? Create a digital kaleidoscope or tessellation? I'm a huge dreamer, and it is often hard to keep my feet headed in a single direction." If you want to find links to the many facets of Crystal, visit her main website at http://www.crystal-writer.com

Emeka Nwakuche lives in Illorin, Kwara State in Nigeria, West Africa, with his wife, where he works as a Doctor of Veterinary Medicine. He is a young writer Harriet E. Michael has mentored long distance, and he has had several devotional pieces published in *The Upper Room* magazine.

Tope Omoniyi holds a Bachelor of Theology and a Masters of Business Administration. She is currently pursuing a Masters in Discipleship and Family Ministries at the Southern Baptist Theological Seminary in Louisville, Kentucky. Previously, she worked for Proctor and Gamble as a marketing associate manager. While living in Nigeria, she authored a book and several articles for different publications. Currently, she coordinates a Family and Marital Clinic which holds a Facebook Live broadcast every Sunday at 2:30 EST where she speaks on Marriage and Family. She and her husband live in Louisville where they both attend Southern Seminary.

Deborah Aubrey-Peyron lives in a small town in Southern Indiana with her husband, Mark. They have three sons, Ben, David, and Andy, daughters-in-law, and grandchildren. They have been members of Covenant Prayer Group at St. Mary's Catholic Church in Lanesville, Indiana, for over 25 years. Mr. and Mrs. Peyron served two terms on the board of Directors for Lifeline Outreach Ministries, with Pastor Ivie Dennis. Mrs.

Peyron is an author and evangelist for the gospel of Jesus Christ. She has written 15 books, including the Miraculous Interventions book series, *Let's Take a Walk, Dave, Christmas Chaos!* book and coloring book, *Deb's Christmas Cookbook*, and others. Her first two books in the Miraculous Interventions series were accepted in the Vatican Library in Rome, Italy. Deborah also edits for other authors, works part-time in the medical field, and still finds time for God, Mark, (husband and love of her life) children, grandchildren, and extended family, or like-family members. A life well-lived is a life well-loved.

Ron Wasson was born in Nigeria, West Africa, the son of missionaries. He currently lives in Heath, Texas. Married thirty-eight years, he and his wife, Rhonda, have two daughters and two grandchildren. Ron writes articles, devotions, and stories for anthologies. His work has appeared in *Chicken Soup for the Soul*, *Among Worlds* magazine, *SEEK* magazine, *Power for Living*, *The Secret Place*, and *The Upper Room* devotional magazine. When he is not writing, he enjoys working in his yard and playing with his grandchildren.

Debbie Lynn Wells was born in Ohio, moved to Michigan, and then to Louisville, Kentucky where she currently resides. She has worn many hats in her life working in communications, payroll, and receiving for various companies in Ohio, Michigan, and Kentucky. She considered her most important role to have been that of caregiver to her mother after her father passed away. She has written stories, songs, and poems since childhood. She also enjoys photography. She is a member of Louisville Christian Writers (LCW).

Recommended Resources

Books about Prayer

A Call to Prayer – J. C. Ryle

A Call to Spiritual Reformation: Priorities from Paul and His Prayer – D. A. Carson

A Woman's Call to Prayer: Making Your Desire to Pray a Reality – Elizabeth George

Disciplines of a Godly Man – R. Kent Hughes

Hudson Taylor's Spiritual Secret – Dr. Hudson Taylor

Life and Diary of David Brainerd – Edited: Jonathan Edwards

Pray About Everything: Cultivating God-Dependency – Paul Tautges

Prayer: Experiencing Awe and Intimacy with God – Tim Keller

Prayer: It's Not About You – Harriet E. Michael

    Study Guide on Prayer—A Companion to Prayer: It's Not About You – Shirley Crowder

Praying Backwards – Bryan Chapell

Praying the Bible – Donald S. Whitney

Praying the Names of God – Ann Spangler

Reaching the Ear of God: Praying More and More Like Jesus – Wayne A. Mack

Spurgeon on Prayer – Charles Spurgeon

The Autobiography of George Muller – George Muller

The Complete Works of E. M. Bounds on Prayer – E. M. Bounds

The Heart of Prayer – Jerram Barrs

With Christ in the School of Prayer – Andrew Murray

With the Master: On Our Knees – Susan J. Heck

Devotionals

A Shelter in the Time of Storm: Meditations on God and Trouble – Paul David Tripp

Cross Talking: A Daily Gospel for Transforming Addicts – Mark E. Shaw

Glimpses of Prayer – Shirley Crowder & Harriet E. Michael

Glimpses of the Savior – Shirley Crowder & Harriet E. Michael

Hearing and Answering God: Praying Psalms 1-75 – Stephen D. Cloud

Hearing and Answering God: Praying Psalms 76-150 – Stephen D. Cloud

Hope for New Beginnings – Dr. Howard Eyrich & Shirley Crowder

My Utmost for His Highest – Oswald Chambers

New Morning Mercies: A Daily Gospel Devotional – Paul David Tripp

The Quiet Place: Daily Devotional Readings – Nancy DeMoss Walgemuth

Through Baca's Valley – J. C. Philpot

Valley of Vision: A Collection of Puritan Prayers – Arthur G. Bennett

Whiter Than Snow: Meditations on Sin and Mercy – Paul David Tripp

Also by the Compilers

By: Harriet E. Michael & Shirley Crowder

Glimpses of Prayer

One of the primary means Christ-followers communicate with God is through prayer. The other is the Word of God—the Bible. God is looking for prayer warriors—men and women who will call on Him and stand in the gap before Him lifting up situations, circumstances, praises, catastrophes, and concerns in their prayers.

This ten-week devotional is centered around prayer. Each devotion focuses on verses in the Bible that speak about prayer. Harriet E. Michael wrote the devotions from the Old Testament, and Shirley Crowder wrote the devotions from the New Testament. The devotional weeks alternate between the New Testament and the Old Testament.

Available on Kindle and in paperback from Amazon and most bookstores by request.

Glimpses of the Savior: 50 Meditations for Thanksgiving, Christmas, and the New Year Finding Jesus Among the Celebrations and Decorations

In early November, we get busy preparing for Thanksgiving, Christmas, and the New Year, and we often forget the real meanings behind these celebrations.

We can guard against this by preparing our hearts to seek Him as we focus on God's Word and by remembering that

Thanksgiving is a time to give God thanks; Christmas is the celebration of the Savior's birth; the New Year brings new beginnings. Then, as we go about doing the things the Lord has called us to do where He has called us to do them, we catch Glimpses of the Savior and biblical truth in the things we experience and observe.

These devotionals are based on memories of Thanksgiving, Christmas, and New Year Celebrations in Africa and America. May the Holy Spirit work through these meditations to help readers recognize Glimpses of the Savior in the things they observe and become skilled at finding Jesus among the celebrations and decorations.

Available on Kindle and in paperback from Amazon and most bookstores by request.

By: Harriet E. Michael

Prayer: It's Not About You

Is prayer a mighty spiritual weapon or a waste of time? Is it something to be engaged in fiercely, as if wielding a weapon in the midst of a spiritual battle, or is it just a personal practice to achieve a calmer, more focused and disciplined life? Does prayer really change anything?

Those questions and so many more are discussed inside the pages of this book. The book does not simply offer one writer's perspective on the topic of prayer. Instead, it delves deep into Scripture to see how prayer is presented in God's Word.

The book offers a thorough study of prayer from a Biblical

perspective. Moving from Genesis to Revelation, this book looks at instances of prayer as recorded in the Bible, exploring the who, what, where, when, how, and why.

Available on Kindle and in paperback from Amazon and most bookstores by request.

By: Shirley Crowder

Study Guide on Prayer—A Companion to Prayer: It's Not About You

This study guide is designed to help you study, individually or in a group setting, the book, *Prayer: It's Not About You*. As you work your way through this study guide, you will read the book chapter by chapter. Then you will be guided to interact with the teachings, principles, and practices contained in Scripture and *Prayer: It's Not About You*.

It is the author's prayer that as you work through this study guide you will gain knowledge and understanding, through the work of the Holy Spirit, that will lead you to incorporate the teachings, principles, and practices in the book into your prayer life so that as your passion to pray increases, it will result in a strengthened relationship with God the Father, through Jesus Christ His Son.

Available on Kindle and in paperback from Amazon and most bookstores by request.

Also from Write Integrity Press

In this first book in the "Hope Rising Bible Series," Andrea Thom digs deep into the truths found in the book of Ruth. Her discoveries encourage women seeking meaning from difficult times and direction in the path on which the Lord has placed them.

Bolivian Missionary, Peggy Cunningham blesses women with her devotions from a unique perspective. DANCING LIKE BEES was created as the author rested on God through a difficult time.

SHAPE YOUR SOUL is her stirring collection of devotions focused on strengthening faith, amping up joy, and even building physical as well as the spiritual muscle!

**Thank you
for reading our books!**

**Look for other books
published by**

Pix-N-Pens Publishing
An imprint of Write Integrity Press
www.WriteIntegrity.com

Made in the USA
Columbia, SC
15 November 2018